Let's Make Cute Stuff by Aranzi Aronzo!

Cute Stuff

Contents

Hi, we're Aranzi Aronzo.
This book contains
instructions on
how to make things
that you'll want to take
around with you
every single day:
bags, little things to put
inside your bags,
things to wear, and more.
Just carrying
cute stuff around
can make you feel happy.
Try to make them
while imagining
the wonderful times
you'll have carrying
them around!

Before You Start

Oh, I really ought to read this beforehand or something terrible could happen!

White Rabbit
Carefree. She loves to eat, have fun, and sleep.
Not so good with the handicrafts.
She's best friends with Brown Bunny.

Make sure you read this before you start. You'll definitely be glad you did.

Brown Bunny
She's cool, smart, and responsible.
She has a knack for handicrafts.
She sort of talks like an old lady, though.
She's best friends with White Rabbit.

Frequently Used Materials and Tools

Scissors
To cut patterns, cloth, felt, and thread

Sewing Needle
Used when sewing by hand
No particular length or thickness required
Use what works best for you

Regular Thread
Standard No. 60 machine thread
Used to sew cloth
You can use it to sew by hand or by machine
Choose colors close to the colors of the fabrics

Glue
To glue on eyes, noses, and mouths
You can use either cloth glue or wood glue

Embroidery Needle
For French Knot or straight stitches using 3 or 6 threads
It is thicker and has a larger eye than the sewing needle

Embroidery Thread
Used to make eyes, noses, and mouths for the appliqués
Also used for cross-stitching (though you can use regular thread for cross-stitching as well)

Chalk Pencils
Chalk pencils are used to outline your patterns
Use light pencils for dark fabrics and dark pencils for light fabrics so that they stand out
Chalk pencils are useful because you can erase them even if you mess up
A simple colored pencil will do if you don't have a chalk pencil

If you have one
Sewing Machine
If you have a sewing machine at home and can use it, we recommend you do so
You'll be able to work quickly with nice results

Stretch Thread
Use No. 50 sewing thread (e.g. polyester or nylon)
Jersey and fleece stretch when you pull them, so this thread is well suited for them
Choose colors close to the fabric colors

If you have one
Overlock Machine
Fabric won't fray if you sew around the edges with an overlock machine

Ruler
Used to measure lengths when making patterns for bags, pouches, or purses

Awl
Handy for turning the corners of bags, pouches, and purses right side out

Fabric
You can use the fabrics and colors specified in the respective "Materials" sections, or you can use fabrics and colors of your own choice
No one will get angry with you
Use the fabric of your choice!

04

What's a zipper?
What's tape?
What's cord?
How and where do I start preparing?
I have no idea what to do.

All of that stuff is sold at crafts stores. Prepare by trying to read the instructions carefully.

Occasionally Used Materials

Zipper

If it says, "Prepare a 10 cm zipper"

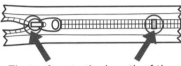

O That refers to the length of the portion that can be opened (to the "bottom stop")

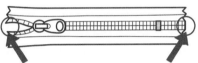

X It doesn't refer to the length of the zipper from end to end

Tape

How to "Make a tape 2 cm wide and 30 cm long"

The crafts store will have rolls of tape in various colors. Choose a roll in a color you like that's 2 cm wide and say, "Please give me 30 cm of this," and they'll cut it for you (Some stores may require you to buy at least 50 cm or some other predetermined length. Tough luck.)

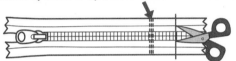

Cord

How to "Prepare 45 cm of a 0.5 cm-thick cord"

Choose a roll in a color you like that's 0.5 cm thick and say, "Please give me 45 cm of this," and they'll cut it for you (Some stores may require you to buy at least 50 cm or some other predetermined length. Tough luck.)

How to "Prepare a 10 cm zipper"

① Pick out a zipper and tell the person at the crafts store, "Please make it 10 cm long," and they'll attach the bottom stop at the right length (Sometimes they can't do it. Tough luck.)

② Buy a bottom stop and attach it at the proper position to create the desired length

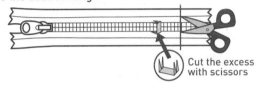

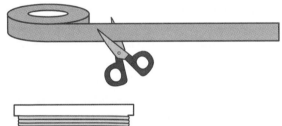

Cut the excess with scissors

③ If you don't have a bottom stop, closely sew back and forth three times by hand or by machine at the desired length

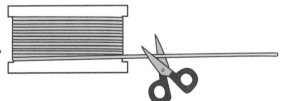

How To Make Patterns

Enlarge or trace the pattern, or make your own with a ruler, then cut Your pattern is done

① If you need to enlarge to get the ideal size

Copy Machine

Enlarge to the ratio specified on the "Patterns" page

② If there's no need to enlarge because the pattern is already at 100%

White of eyes
White felt
Pupils
Brown felt
Mouth
White felt
Never-ending drops of sweat
White felt

Create the pattern by placing a thin piece of paper on top of the book and tracing it with a pencil You can also create a pattern by making a photocopy at 100%

③ If the pattern is a square or rectangle, as with bags, pouches, and purses

You can make the pattern by measuring with a ruler instead of copying or enlarging

You can enlarge or reduce to ratios not specified in this book. Appliqués are especially fun to make in various sizes.

Brown Bunny! I made the pattern. What's next? What do I do?

Next we trace the pattern onto the fabric.

Tracing Pattern Onto Fabric

① Place pattern on fabric
② Trace using chalk pencil

Pattern

③ Cut fabric as traced

"Zig-zag" and "overlock" are such cool names. But what on earth do they mean?

"Zig-zag machine" and "overlock machine" are hardworking machines.

Zig-zag Machine and Overlock Machine

Fabric that frays easily can start to look like this along the edges after you cut it into patterns
Let's keep that from happening

If you're the kind of person who doesn't care whether it frays or not, you can just sew the patterns together without any further steps
It's not like it will fray that quickly, so as long as you're not bothered by it, it's not a big deal

How to "Keep fabric that frays easily from fraying"

① Do a zig-zag stitch around the edges if your machine has a zig-zag function

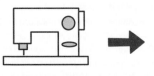

② Do an overlock stitch if you have an overlock machine

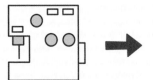

③ If you have neither a zig-zag machine nor an overlock machine, apply sealant along the edges to prevent them from fraying

Fabric sealant is sold in crafts stores
If you seal the edges, the fabric will harden and won't easily fray
Read the instructions carefully when using the fabric sealant

   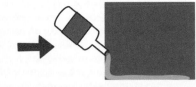

Have fun making this stuff however you like! No one will get angry at you if you make a mistake.

You don't have to use the fabrics or colors we suggest, or even follow our directions exactly. Better to use the fabrics you have around the house to make things in the way that's easiest for you.

How To Sew

When Sewing By Machine

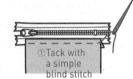

Do a straight stitch using the machine
It's good if you have a machine at home and can use it, because machines can sew faster and more neatly

When Sewing By Hand

Do a backstitch or close blind stitch when sewing by hand

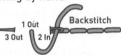

It's better not to use a machine for hard-to-reach places like around a zipper. Just sew those by hand.

Machine and hand sewing

When it says to "sew along the dotted line," you can do it either by machine or by hand
Either is fine

Tacking

A tack is when you do a simple blind stitch before doing the final stitch by hand or machine
If you tack first it'll come out more neatly, without getting twisted or out of position

① Tack with a simple blind stitch

② Final stitch

③ Remove tacking thread after the final stitch

1 Strand, 3 Strands, 6 Strands

Threading one thread through your needle: "1 strand"
Threading three strands of embroidery thread through your embroidery needle: "3 strands"
Threading six strands of embroidery thread through your embroidery needle: "6 strands"
So what do we mean by "5 strands"?—I'm sure you can guess!

Tie end of 1 thread / Tie ends of 3 threads / Tie ends of 6 threads / Tie both ends of 3 threads

1 strand
Thread one thread through sewing needle

3 strands
Thread 3 threads through embroidery needle

6 strands
Thread 6 threads through embroidery needle
You can also thread 3 threads and tie both ends

Various Sewing And Stitching Techniques

Cross-stitch

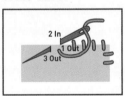

FN Stitch (French Knot Stitch)

Turn twice / Turn 3 times

① When Making a Double French Knot
Wrap thread around needle twice
When Making a Triple French Knot
Wrap thread around needle three times

② With thread still wrapped around the needle, pierce fabric right next to where the thread comes out

③ Ta-da!
Often used for making eyes and noses

Overlock

View from side / View from top

You do an overlock stitch when you sew two pieces of fabric together

S-Stitch (Straight Stitch)

Bend slightly / Bend slightly

Make a straight line
Often used for making mouths

You can create smiling faces and other curvy lines by loosening an S-Stitch and applying glue to the back of the thread with a thin stick (like a toothpick, for example)

Make a lot of cute stuff and make everyone jealous!

You'll have a lot of fun both making and using cute stuff. Make cute stuff and enjoy a happy everyday life!

They're Long Doll Bags because
their torsos are long and they're bags.
When you walk around with them,
they dangle along with you.
White Rabbit and Panda recommend
that you take to setting out with
Long Doll Bags dangling from your arms.

How to Make Long Doll Bags

01

Cut fabric and felt according to the patterns

02

Cut fabric and felt according to the patterns

03
Stack halves of ears inside out and sew along the dotted red lines

Reverse / White thread / Reverse / Black thread

04
Turn ears right side out and stuff in a bit of cotton
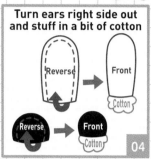
Reverse → Front / Cotton
Reverse → Front / Cotton

05
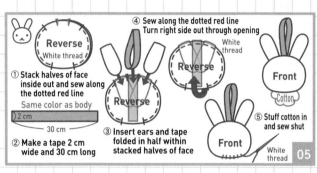
① Stack halves of face inside out and sew along the dotted red line
Same color as body
2 cm / 30 cm
② Make a tape 2 cm wide and 30 cm long
③ Insert ears and tape folded in half within stacked halves of face
④ Sew along the dotted red line. Turn right side out through opening
⑤ Stuff cotton in and sew shut
Reverse / White thread / Reverse / White thread / Front / Cotton / Front / White thread

06
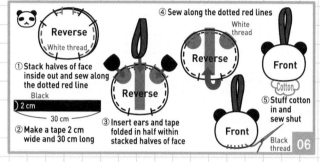
① Stack halves of face inside out and sew along the dotted red line
Black
2 cm / 30 cm
② Make a tape 2 cm wide and 30 cm long
③ Insert ears and tape folded in half within stacked halves of face
④ Sew along the dotted red lines
⑤ Stuff cotton in and sew shut
Reverse / White thread / White thread / Reverse / Front / Cotton / Front / Black thread

07
Stack halves of arms and legs inside out and sew along the dotted red line
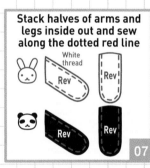
White thread / Rev / Rev / Rev / Rev

08
Turn ears right side out and stuff in a bit of cotton

Stuff / Cotton / Front / Stuff / Front / Stuff / Cotton / Front / Stuff / Cotton / Front / Stuff

09
If your fabric frays easily, sew edges with zig-zag or overlock machine
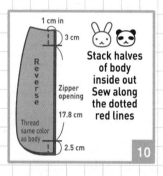
Prepare a zipper the same color as body
17 cm

10
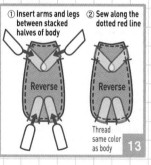
1 cm in / 3 cm / Reverse / Zipper opening / 17.8 cm / Thread same color as body / 2.5 cm
Stack halves of body inside out. Sew along the dotted red lines

11
① Open toward reverse, fold sides 1 cm
1 cm / Fold 1 cm / Fold 1 cm / Reverse
It will come out neater if you iron it first

② Turn right side out, place on zipper
Front
Line up zipper and middle of body

③ Tack around zipper opening
Front / Tack about 0.5 cm

④ Sew along the dotted red line
Remove tacking thread after sewing
Sew about 0.5 cm in / Front
Thread same color as body

12
Stack halves of body inside out and sew along the dotted red line
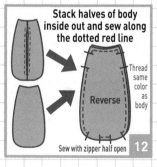
Reverse / Thread same color as body
Sew with zipper half open

13
① Insert arms and legs between stacked halves of body
② Sew along the dotted red line

Reverse / Reverse / Thread same color as body

14
Turn inside side out through zipper opening
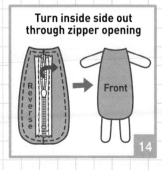
Reverse → Front

15
Sew head and body together
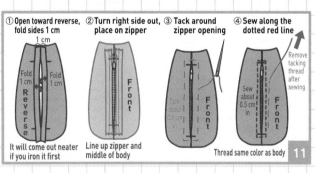
White thread

16
Position eyes, nose, mouth; glue lightly before doing cross-stitch

Make me look handsome.
Black thread / Brown thread

17

Nice, huh?
Isn't it?
Done

Long Doll Bag Materials

Chalk pencils

Scissors

Glue

Iron

Sewing machine

If you have one
Overlock machine

Fabric of your choice
- 🐰 White and color of body
- 🐼 White and black

Felt
- 🐰 Brown
- 🐼 Black

Regular thread
- 🐰 White and brown and color of body
- 🐼 White and black

Zipper
About 17 cm
- 🐰 Same color as body
- 🐼 White

2 cm-wide tape, 30 cm long
- 🐰 Same color as body
- 🐼 Black

Cotton

Sewing needle

Ruler

Long Doll Bag Patterns

Enlarge to 120% for the ideal size

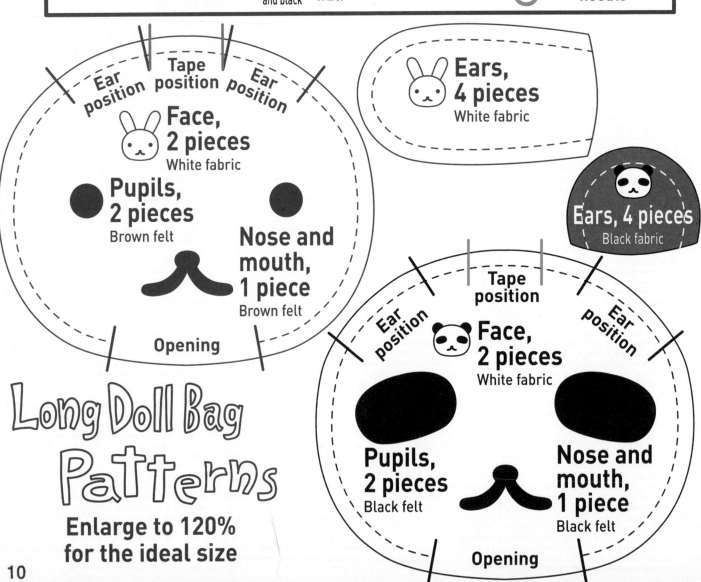

Ear position Tape position Ear position

Face, 2 pieces
White fabric

Pupils, 2 pieces
Brown felt

Nose and mouth, 1 piece
Brown felt

Opening

Ears, 4 pieces
White fabric

Ears, 4 pieces
Black fabric

Ear position Tape position Ear position

Face, 2 pieces
White fabric

Pupils, 2 pieces
Black felt

Nose and mouth, 1 piece
Black felt

Opening

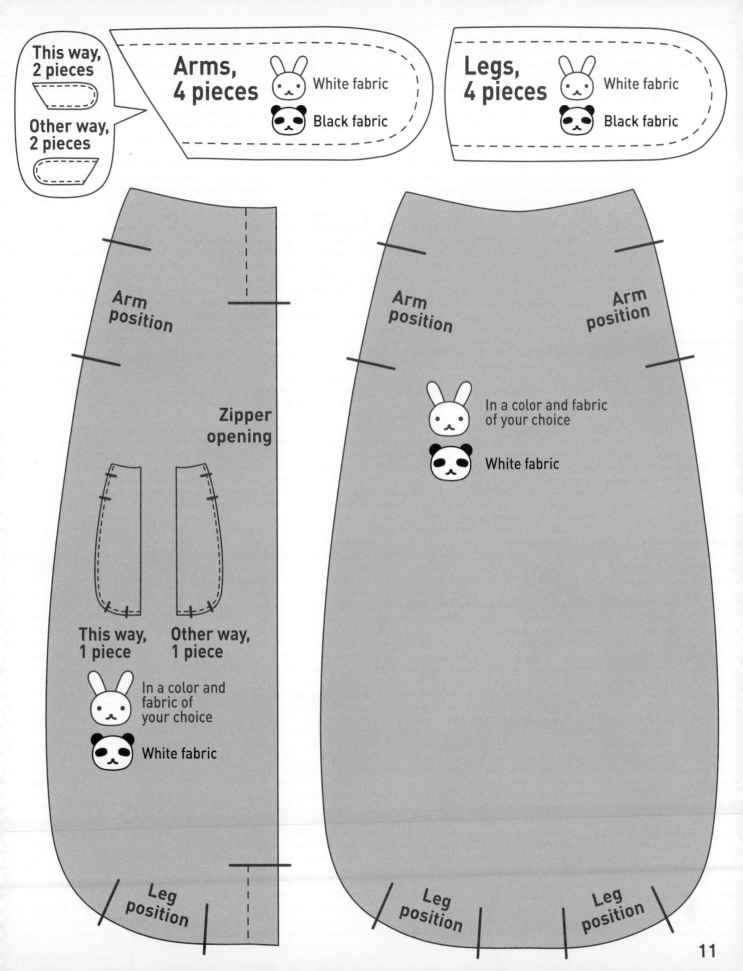

This way, 2 pieces

Other way, 2 pieces

Arms, 4 pieces
🐰 White fabric
🐼 Black fabric

Legs, 4 pieces
🐰 White fabric
🐼 Black fabric

Arm position

Zipper opening

🐰 In a color and fabric of your choice
🐼 White fabric

This way, 1 piece

Other way, 1 piece

🐰 In a color and fabric of your choice
🐼 White fabric

Arm position

Arm position

Leg position

Leg position

Leg position

If you have a Bunny or Squirrel hair band, people will probably say, "Oh, that's so cute!"
If you have a Liar or Sprite hair band, they'll probably think, "That's funny," or "Weird!"

How To Make a Bear Hair Band

Cut felt according to the patterns

Patterns
Pattern at 100%

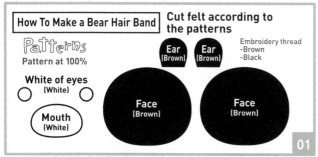

White of eyes (White)

Mouth (White)

Ear (Brown) Ear (Brown)

Face (Brown) Face (Brown)

Embroidery thread
-Brown
-Black

01

Glue whites of eyes and mouth

02

Pupils: FN Stitch, turn twice
Black thread, 6 strands

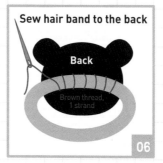

Nose: Black thread, 3 strands
FN Stitch, turn twice

03

Black thread, 3 strands
Mouth: S-Stitch

1 2 3 4 5

04

Insert ears and overlock stitch

Cotton

Brown thread, 1 strand

Stuff cotton and sew shut

05

Sew hair band to the back

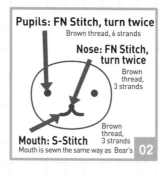

Back

Brown thread, 1 strand

06

You can also enlarge your pattern and make a bigger Bear

Isn't it easy?

Done!

07

How To Make a White Rabbit Hair Band

Cut felt according to the patterns

Patterns
Pattern at 100%

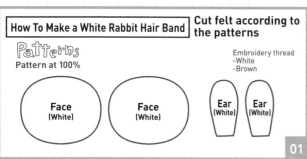

Face (White) Face (White)

Ear (White) Ear (White)

Embroidery thread
-White
-Brown

01

Pupils: FN Stitch, turn twice
Brown thread, 6 strands

Nose: FN Stitch, turn twice
Brown thread, 3 strands

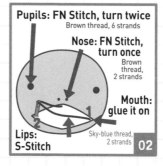

Brown thread, 3 strands

Mouth: S-Stitch
Mouth is sewn the same way as Bear's

02

Insert ears and overlock stitch
Stuff cotton and sew shut

Back

White thread, 1 strand

Cotton

Done!

03

How To Make a Sprite Hair Band

Cut felt according to the patterns

Patterns
Pattern at 100%

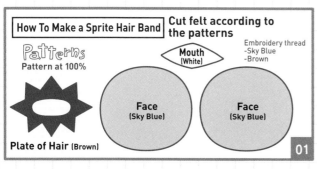

Mouth (White)

Plate of Hair (Brown)

Face (Sky Blue) Face (Sky Blue)

Embroidery thread
-Sky Blue
-Brown

01

Pupils: FN Stitch, turn twice
Brown thread, 6 strands

Nose: FN Stitch, turn once
Brown thread, 2 strands

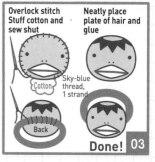

Mouth: glue it on

Lips: S-Stitch
2 1
Sky-blue thread, 2 strands

02

Overlock stitch
Stuff cotton and sew shut

Neatly place plate of hair and glue

Cotton
Sky-blue thread, 1 strand

Back

Done!

03

How To Make a Squirrel Hair Band

Cut felt according to the patterns

Patterns
Pattern at 100%

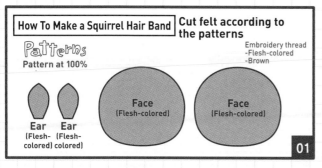

Ear (Flesh-colored) Ear (Flesh-colored)

Face (Flesh-colored) Face (Flesh-colored)

Embroidery thread
-Flesh-colored
-Brown

01

Pupils: FN Stitch, turn twice
Brown thread, 6 strands

Nose: FN Stitch, turn twice
Brown thread, 3 strands

Brown thread, 3 strands

Mouth: S-Stitch
Mouth is sewn the same way as Bear's

02

Insert ears and overlock stitch
Stuff cotton and sew shut

Draw stripes with brown pencil

Flesh-colored thread, 1 strand

Cotton

Back

Done!

03

Hair Band Materials

 Chalk pencils

 **Scissors**

 Glue

 **Embroidery needle** Used to sew FN and S-Stitches for eyes, noses, etc.

 **Sewing needle** Used for overlock stitching and sewing faces to bands

 Felt Respective colors

 Embroidery thread Respective colors

Cotton

 **Hair bands** In your favorite colors

How to Make Hair Bands and Patterns

How To Make a Spritekin Hair Band — Cut felt according to the patterns

Patterns Pattern at 100%

Mouth (White)

Embroidery thread -White -Brown

Face (Light Green)

Face (Light Green)

Plate of Hair (Light Orange)

01

Glue mouth
Pupils: FN Stitch, turn twice — Brown thread, 6 strands

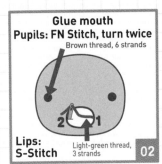

Lips: S-Stitch — Light-green thread, 3 strands

02

Overlock stitch Stuff cotton and sew shut

Neatly place plate of hair and glue

Light-green thread, 1 strand

Cotton

Back

Sprrr! 03

How To Make a White Sheep Hair Band — Cut felt according to the patterns

Patterns Pattern at 100%

Embroidery thread -Flesh-colored -Black

Horns (White)

Face (Flesh-colored)

Face (Flesh-colored)

01

Pupils: FN Stitch, turn twice — Black thread, 6 strands

Mouth: S-Stitch Black thread, 3 strands

Nose: FN Stitch, turn twice Black thread, 3 strands

Cut notch as indicated

02

Insert horns and overlock stitch Stuff cotton and sew shut

Back

Flesh-colored thread, 1 strand

Cotton

Put on both White Sheep and Black Sheep, bah! 03

How To Make a Black Sheep Hair Band — Cut felt according to the patterns

Patterns Pattern at 100%

Embroidery thread -Black

Horns (White)

Face (Black)

Face (Black)

White of eyes (White)

01

Glue white of eyes
Pupils: FN Stitch, turn twice — Black thread, 6 strands

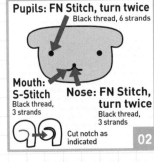

Cut notch as indicated

02

Insert horns and overlock stitch Stuff cotton and sew shut

Back

Black thread, 1 strand

Cotton

Done, bah! 03

How To Make a Bad Guy Hair Band

Patterns Pattern at 100%

Cut felt according to the patterns

Embroidery thread
-Black

Mouth
(White)

Face (Black)

White of eyes (White)

Face (Black)

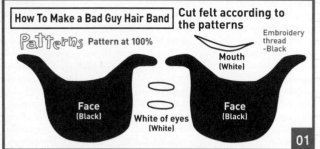 **01**

Glue white of eyes and mouth
Pupils: FN Stitch, turn twice

Black thread, 6 strands

 **02**

Overlock stitch
Stuff cotton and sew shut

Black thread, 1 strand

Cotton

Back

Make 10 and put them all on! Cool!

 **03**

How To Make a Liar Hair Band

Patterns Pattern at 100%

Cut felt according to the patterns

White of eye (White)

Embroidery thread
-Yellow
-Black

Face (Yellow)

Face (Yellow)

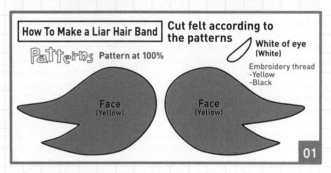 **01**

Glue white of eye and mouth
Pupil: FN Stitch, turn twice

Black thread, 6 strands

 **02**

Overlock stitch
Stuff cotton and sew shut

Cotton

Yellow thread, 1 strand

The boys will *love* you if you put me on...

 **03**

How To Make a Panda Hair Band

Patterns Pattern at 100%

Cut felt according to the patterns

Ear (Black) Ear (Black)

Embroidery thread
-White
-Black

Eye (Black) Eye (Black)

Face (White)

Face (White)

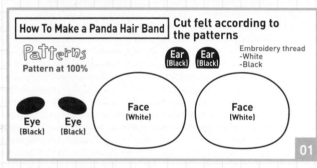 **01**

Glue on eyes
Nose: FN Stitch, turn twice

Black thread, 3 strands

Mouth: S-Stitch
Black thread, 3 strands
Mouth is sewn the same way as Bear's

 **02**

Insert ears and overlock stitch
Stuff cotton and sew shut

Back

White thread, 1 strand

It's done

 **03**

How To Make a Pinkie Hair Band

Patterns Pattern at 100%

Cut felt according to the patterns

White of eyes (White)

Embroidery thread
-Pink
-Black

Ear (Pink) Ear (Pink)

Face (Pink)

Face (Pink)

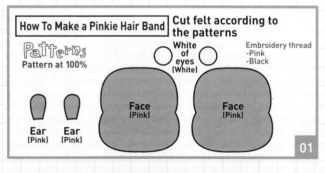 **01**

Glue white of eyes

Eyelashes: S-Stitch
Black thread, 3 strands

Pupils: FN Stitch, turn 3 times
Black thread, 6 strands

Mouth: S-Stitch
Black thread, 3 strands

Nose: FN Stitch, turn twice
Black thread, 3 strands

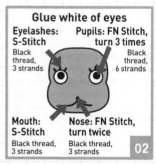 **02**

Insert ears and overlock stitch
Stuff cotton and sew shut

Back

Pink thread, 1 strand

Cotton

Pinkie loooves Pink! Even her hair band is pink!

 **03**

How To Make a Terry Hair Band

Patterns Pattern at 100%

Cut felt according to the patterns

Embroidery thread
-White
-Brown

Ear (Brown) Ear (Brown)

Face (White)

Face (White)

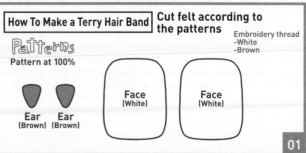 **01**

Eyes: S-Stitch
Brown thread, 3 strands

Nose: FN Stitch, turn twice
Brown thread, 6 strands

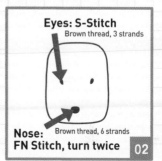 **02**

Overlock stitch
Stuff cotton and sew shut

Glue ears

White thread, 1 strand

Cotton

Back

Done, ruff

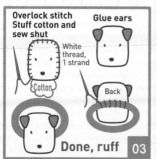 **03**

People are always curious to know what other people are reading.
You might feel relieved to see someone reading a comic book,
or freak out when you see someone reading a difficult-looking book.
Why is that, anyway?
Let's cover our books to keep what we're reading a secret.

How to Make Book Covers

01
Cut fabric according to the pattern
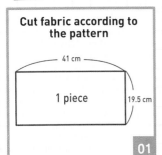
41 cm
1 piece
19.5 cm

02
Sew edges of the fabric with a zig-zag machine or an overlock machine (to prevent the fabric from fraying)

03
Fold left and right edges in 1 cm
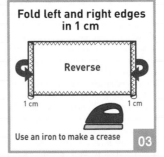
Reverse
1 cm   1 cm
Use an iron to make a crease

04
Sew along the dotted red lines
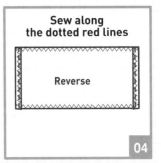
Reverse

05
Fold top and bottom edges in 1 cm
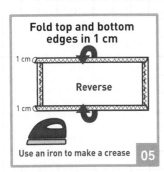
1 cm
Reverse
1 cm
Use an iron to make a crease

06
Fold left and right sides in 7 cm
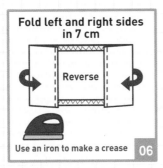
Reverse
Use an iron to make a crease

07
Sew along the dotted red lines
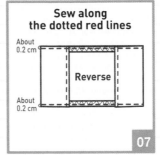
About 0.2 cm
Reverse
About 0.2 cm

08
Attach appliqué
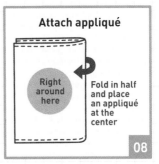
Right around here
Fold in half and place an appliqué at the center

09
Cut appliqué felt according to the patterns

BOOK

10
Decide placement
You should place the book on top of the face to make it look like I'm reading.
You should place the hands on top of the book to make it look like I'm holding the book.

BOOK

11
Glue firmly
If you're worried that gluing isn't enough, put your mind at ease by cross-stitching them on.

BOOK

12
Make eyes and nose with embroidery thread
Make the pupils with an FN Stitch, turning three times (Brown thread, 6 strands)
Make the nose with an FN Stitch, turning once (Brown thread, 6 strands)

BOOK

13
Cut appliqué felt according to the patterns

BOOK

14
Position and glue firmly
Make the face first
Make pupils with an FN Stitch, turning three times (Brown thread, 6 strands)
Make the nose with an FN Stitch, turning once (Brown thread, 6 strands)

BOOK

15
Cut appliqué felt according to the patterns

BOOK

16
Position and glue firmly

BOOK

17
Cut appliqué felt according to the patterns

BOOK

18
Position and glue firmly
Make pupils with an FN Stitch, turning three times (Black thread, 6 strands)

BOOK

19
Done

BOOK

20
Look smart even if you're reading a comic book.

BOOK

Book Cover Materials

Chalk pencils

Scissors

Glue

Iron

Sewing machine

Overlock machine

If you have one

Fabric for book cover

In a color of your choice
Thin sailcloth or canvas

Regular thread

Same color as fabric

Felt for appliqués
In whatever colors you need

Embroidery thread

Same colors as the appliqué felt

Ruler

Embroidery needle

Used to make eyes and noses for the appliqués

Sewing needle

Used to cross-stitch the appliqués

Book Cover Patterns

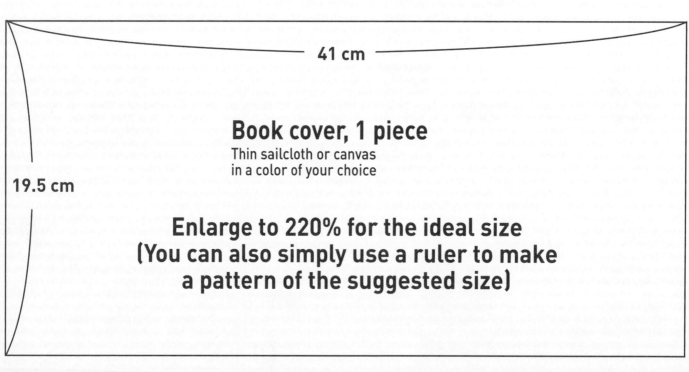

— 41 cm —

19.5 cm

Book cover, 1 piece
Thin sailcloth or canvas
in a color of your choice

**Enlarge to 220% for the ideal size
(You can also simply use a ruler to make
a pattern of the suggested size)**

Book Cover Appliqué Patterns

Patterns at 100% so no need to enlarge

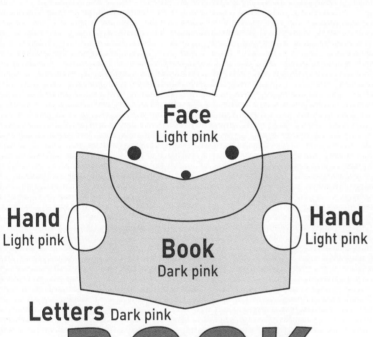

Face Light pink

Hand Light pink

Hand Light pink

Book Dark pink

Letters Dark pink

BOOK

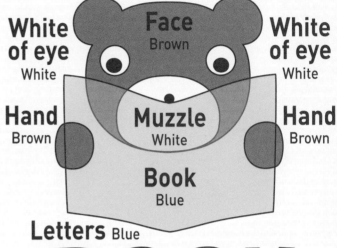

White of eye White

Face Brown

White of eye White

Hand Brown

Muzzle White

Hand Brown

Book Blue

Letters Blue

BOOK

All appliqués are felt

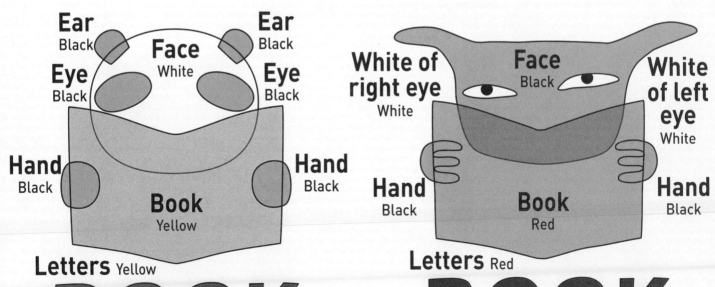

Ear Black

Ear Black

Face White

Eye Black

Eye Black

Hand Black

Hand Black

Book Yellow

Letters Yellow

BOOK

White of right eye White

Face Black

White of left eye White

Hand Black

Hand Black

Book Red

Letters Red

BOOK

At school, you need purses of various sizes
for all sorts of things: your lunch box,
your gym shoes, your recorder, etc.
Grown-ups also need purses of various sizes
to organize things within larger bags
and suitcases, when you're traveling, and so on.
Wouldn't it be nice to be able to make purses
in whatever sizes you need?
Let's make purses in whatever sizes you need.

How to Make Assorted Purses

Girls need lots of purses of various sizes. Let's make all the sizes you need.

01

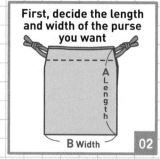

First, decide the length and width of the purse you want

A Length

B Width

02

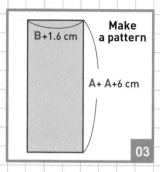

Make a pattern

B+1.6 cm

A+ A+6 cm

03

Trace pattern onto fabric and cut out

04

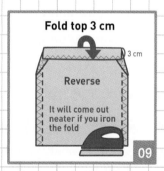

Sew edges of the fabric with a zig-zag machine or an overlock machine (to prevent the fabric from fraying)

05

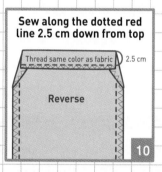

Fold in half inside out

Reverse

06

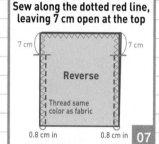

Sew along the dotted red line, leaving 7 cm open at the top

7 cm   7 cm

Reverse

Thread same color as fabric

0.8 cm in   0.8 cm in

07

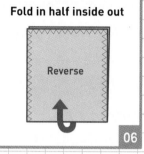

Fold both ends of the top in the direction of the red arrows

About 1 cm

Reverse

It will come out neater if you iron the folds

08

Fold top 3 cm

3 cm

Reverse

It will come out neater if you iron the fold

09

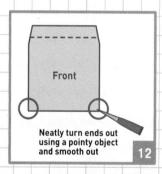

Sew along the dotted red line 2.5 cm down from top

Thread same color as fabric   2.5 cm

Reverse

10

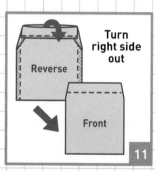

Turn right side out

Reverse

Front

11

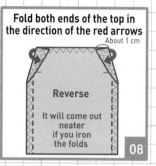

Front

Neatly turn ends out using a pointy object and smooth out

12

When you finish making the purse, thread the drawstring. You can use a cord or make a drawstring from the same fabric as the purse.

13

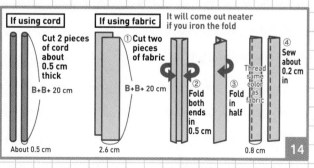

If using cord

Cut 2 pieces of cord about 0.5 cm thick

B+B+ 20 cm

About 0.5 cm

If using fabric

It will come out neater if you iron the fold

① Cut two pieces of fabric

B+B+ 20 cm

2.6 cm

② Fold both ends in 0.5 cm

③ Fold in half

Thread same color as fabric

0.8 cm

④ Sew about 0.2 cm in

14

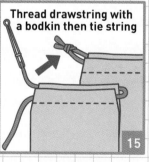

Thread drawstring with a bodkin then tie string

15

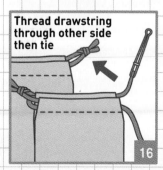

Thread drawstring through other side then tie

16

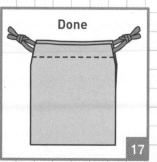

Done

17

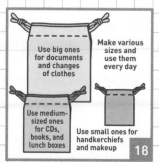

Use big ones for documents and changes of clothes

Make various sizes and use them every day

Use medium-sized ones for CDs, books, and lunch boxes

Use small ones for handkerchiefs and makeup

18

Put on cute appliqués to make unique purses!

See page 72 for appliqués

19

Assorted Purse Materials

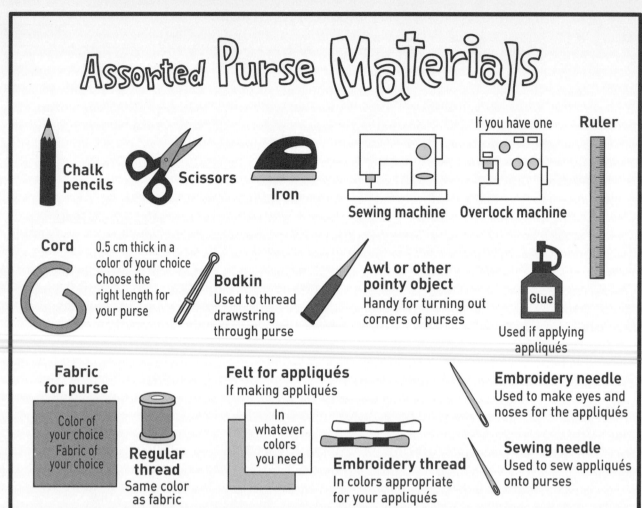

Chalk pencils

Scissors

Iron

Sewing machine

If you have one
Overlock machine

Ruler

Cord
0.5 cm thick in a color of your choice Choose the right length for your purse

Bodkin
Used to thread drawstring through purse

Awl or other pointy object
Handy for turning out corners of purses

Glue
Used if applying appliqués

Fabric for purse
Color of your choice Fabric of your choice

Regular thread
Same color as fabric

Felt for appliqués
If making appliqués
In whatever colors you need

Embroidery thread
In colors appropriate for your appliqués

Embroidery needle
Used to make eyes and noses for the appliqués

Sewing needle
Used to sew appliqués onto purses

Here are some sample sizes for your purses. If you want to make purses in other sizes, read the instructions on page 21 and make your own patterns. Try all sorts of sizes!

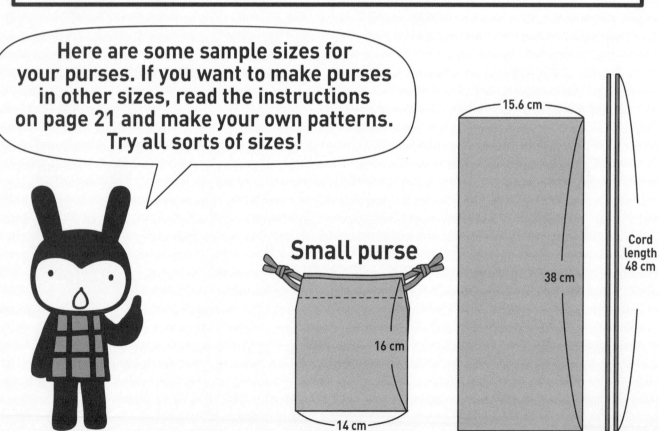

Small purse

15.6 cm

38 cm

16 cm

14 cm

Cord length 48 cm

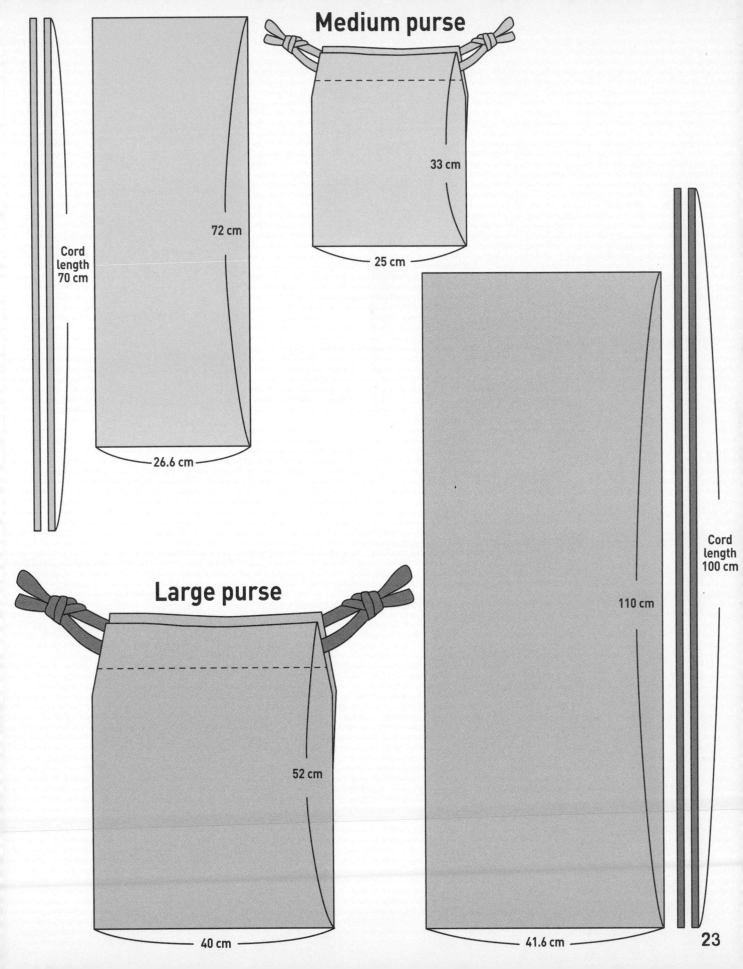

Medium purse

33 cm

25 cm

Cord length 70 cm

72 cm

26.6 cm

Large purse

52 cm

40 cm

Cord length 100 cm

110 cm

41.6 cm

23

As with purses,
you need pouches of various sizes.
Maybe you think pouches are hard to make
because they have zippers.
Well, they're not! You can make them!
Let's make pouches
in whatever sizes you need.

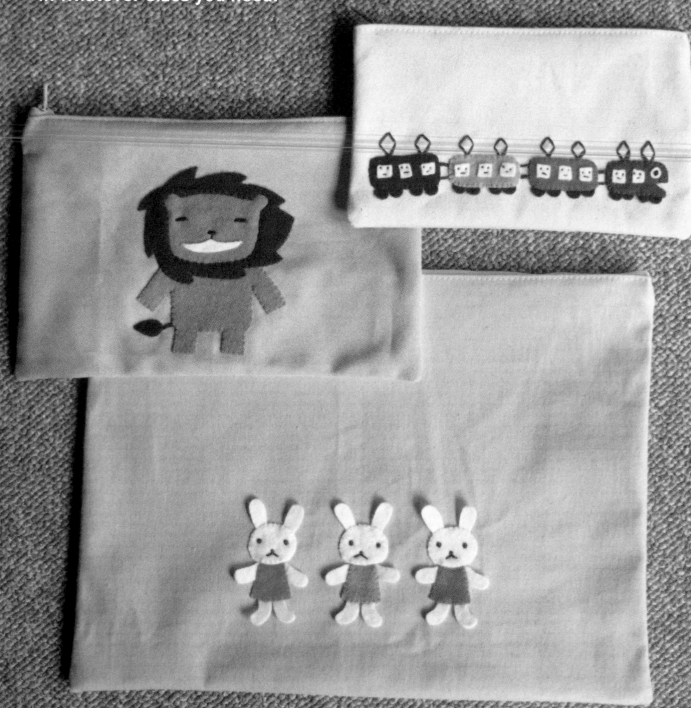

How to Make Assorted Pouches

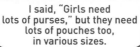

01
I said, "Girls need lots of purses," but they need lots of pouches too, in various sizes.

02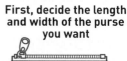
Let's make all the sizes you need.

03
First, decide the length and width of the purse you want
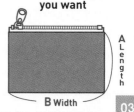
A Length
B Width

04
Make a pattern
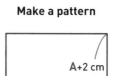 
A+2 cm
B+2 cm

05
Prepare zipper
B-1cm
Read "Zipper" on page 5 if you don't have a zipper of the right length.

06
Cut fabric according to the pattern
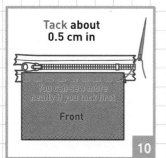
2 pieces

07
Sew edges of the fabric with a zig-zag machine or an overlock machine (to prevent the fabric from fraying)
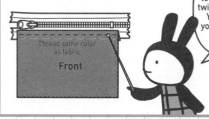

08
Fold top 1 cm back (towards reverse side)

1 cm
Reverse
It'll be easier to sew if you iron the fold first

09
Keeping the top 1 cm folded, place on top of the zipper
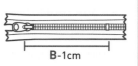
Front

10
Tack about 0.5 cm in
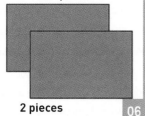
You can sew more neatly if you tack first
Front

11
Sew along the dotted red line, about 0.3 cm in
Thread same color as fabric
Front

It's kind of hard to sew zippers if you're not used to it because they can get twisted or slip out of place. You don't have to force yourself to use a machine: it's fine just to stitch closely by hand.

12
Take out the tacking thread after sewing along the dotted red line
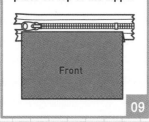
Front

13
Sew the other side the same way
Front
Sew about 0.3 cm in after making a tack
Thread same color as fabric
Front

14
Fold inside out along the zipper
Keep zipper half open
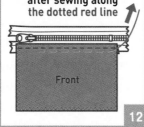
Reverse

15
Sew two halves together along dotted red line

Reverse
Thread same color as fabric
1 cm in
1 cm in
The bumpy metal zipper may make sewing difficult, so don't force yourself to use a machine—just stitch closely by hand

16
Turn right side out through zipper opening
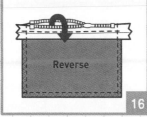
Reverse

17
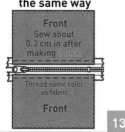
Front
Neatly turn ends out using a pointy object and smooth out

18
Done
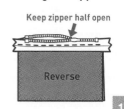
Make pouches of various sizes and use them every day!
You can make them even cuter by putting on appliqués, and cooler by using fabrics with printed patterns

19
This pouch is exactly the size I needed! I couldn't find one to buy! Making them the right size is awesome!

Assorted Pouch Materials

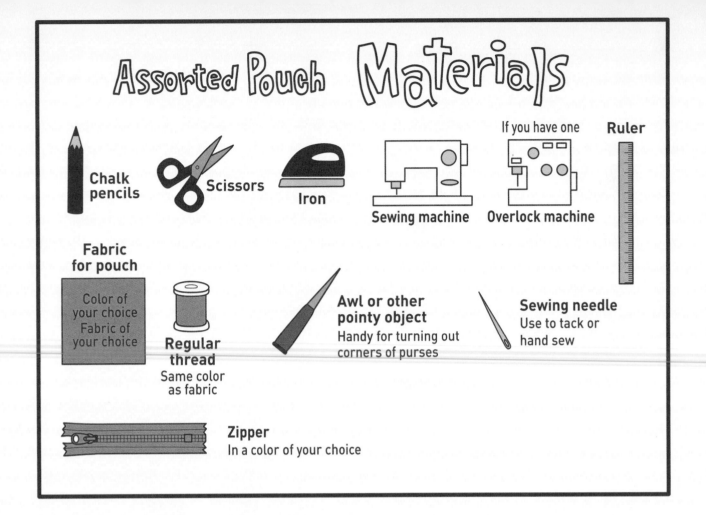

Chalk pencils

Scissors

Iron

Sewing machine

If you have one
Overlock machine

Ruler

Fabric for pouch
Color of your choice
Fabric of your choice

Regular thread
Same color as fabric

Awl or other pointy object
Handy for turning out corners of purses

Sewing needle
Use to tack or hand sew

Zipper
In a color of your choice

Here are some sample sizes for your pouches. If you want to make pouches in other sizes, read the instructions on page 25 and make your own patterns. Make it the size you want, okay?

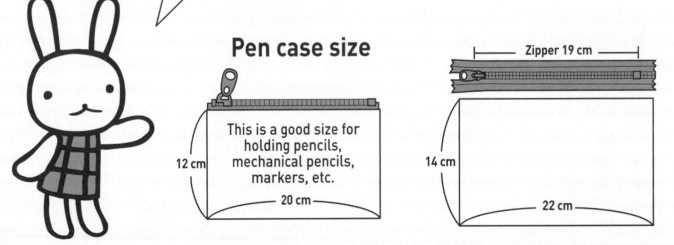

Pen case size

This is a good size for holding pencils, mechanical pencils, markers, etc.

12 cm

20 cm

Zipper 19 cm

14 cm

22 cm

Small Pouch

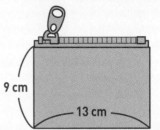

9 cm

13 cm

Good for holding loose change
or credit cards;
also a good size for
makeup, medicine, or stamps

Zipper 12 cm

11 cm

15 cm

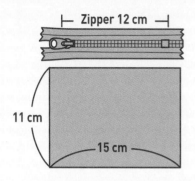

Medium Pouch

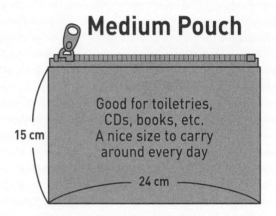

Good for toiletries,
CDs, books, etc.
A nice size to carry
around every day

15 cm

24 cm

Zipper 23 cm

17 cm

26 cm

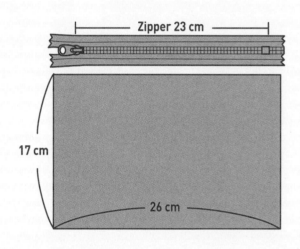

Large pouch

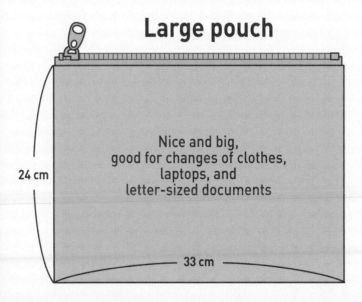

Nice and big,
good for changes of clothes,
laptops, and
letter-sized documents

24 cm

33 cm

Zipper 32 cm

26 cm

35 cm

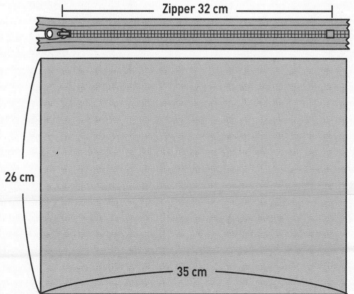

Use Mr. House for your house keys.
Use Mr. Car for your car keys.
Use Mr. Building for your office keys.
Use Mr. Key for all your other keys.
Pretty obvious, right?

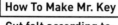 

How to Make Key Rings

How To Make Mr. Key

Cut felt according to the patterns

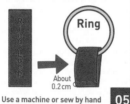

`01`

Glue face onto the "key"

`02`

Glue white of eyes onto the face

`03`

Make pupils and mouth with embroidery thread

Make the pupils with an FN Stitch, turning three times. (Brown thread, 6 strands)

Make the mouth with an S-Stitch (Brown thread, 6 strands)

Thin stick
Loosen the S-Stitch a little. Use the thin stick to apply glue to the back of the thread and fix the mouth into a smile

`04`

Wrap the ring loop around the ring and sew along the dotted red line

Ring

About 0.2 cm

Use a machine or sew by hand

`05`

Insert about 0.8 cm in

Insert the end of the ring loop between the two halves of the key and glue firmly

`06`

Sew along the dotted red line.

Yay, done!

Use a machine, or if sewing by hand, do a close running stitch

Thread same color as felt

`07`

It's fun to put on a bunch!

It's fun to use different colors!

`08`

How To Make Mr. Car

Cut felt according to the patterns

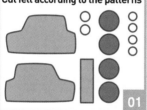

`01`

Glue white of eyes onto the face
Make pupils and mouth

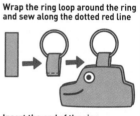

Make pupils with an FN Stitch, turning three times (Brown thread, 6 strands)

Make mouth with an S-Stitch (Brown thread, 6 strands)

Put a face on both sides so you can see it from either direction

`02`

Wrap the ring loop around the ring and sew along the dotted red line

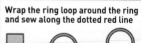

Insert the end of the ring loop between the two halves of the body and glue

`03`

Sew along the dotted red line

Glue wheels onto the body, and hubcaps onto the wheels

Done.

Thread same color as felt

Glue tires firmly on both sides

`04`

How To Make Mr. House

Cut felt according to the patterns

`01`

Glue white of eyes and mouth onto the wall
Make pupils

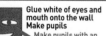

Make pupils with an FN Stitch, turning three times (Brown thread, 6 strands)

Stack walls and glue

Sew along the dotted red line
Thread same color as felt

`02`

Wrap the ring loop around the ring and sew along the dotted white line

Insert the end of the ring loop between the two halves of the roof and glue firmly

`03`

Sew along the dotted white line

Done.

Thread same color as felt

What color's your house?

`04`

How To Make Mr. Building

Cut felt according to the patterns

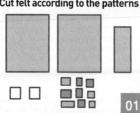

`01`

Glue white of eyes onto the outer wall
Make pupils and mouth with embroidery thread

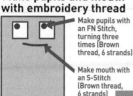

Make pupils with an FN Stitch, turning three times (Brown thread, 6 strands)

Make mouth with an S-Stitch (Brown thread, 6 strands)

`02`

Wrap the ring loop around the ring and sew along the dotted red line

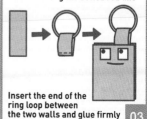

Insert the end of the ring loop between the two walls and glue firmly

`03`

Sew along the dotted red line

Done!

Glue on windows

Thread same color as felt

`04`

Key Ring Materials

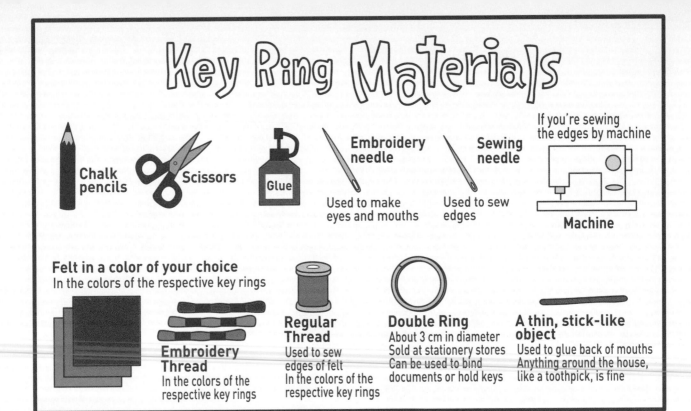

Chalk pencils

Scissors

Glue

Embroidery needle
Used to make eyes and mouths

Sewing needle
Used to sew edges

If you're sewing the edges by machine

Machine

Felt in a color of your choice
In the colors of the respective key rings

Embroidery Thread
In the colors of the respective key rings

Regular Thread
Used to sew edges of felt
In the colors of the respective key rings

Double Ring
About 3 cm in diameter
Sold at stationery stores
Can be used to bind documents or hold keys

A thin, stick-like object
Used to glue back of mouths
Anything around the house, like a toothpick, is fine

Key Ring Patterns

Patterns at 100% so no need to enlarge when copying

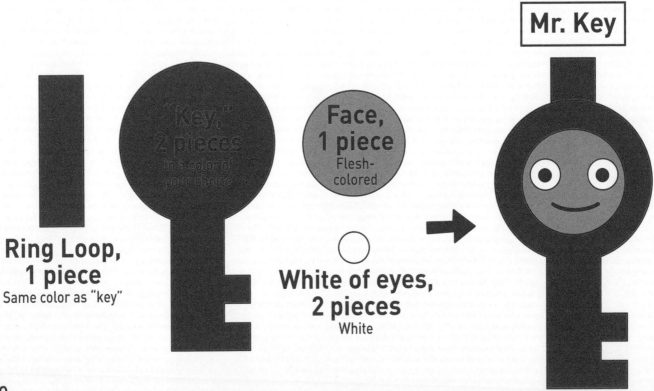

Ring Loop, 1 piece
Same color as "key"

"Key," 2 pieces
In a color of your choice

Face, 1 piece
Flesh-colored

White of eyes, 2 pieces
White

Mr. Key

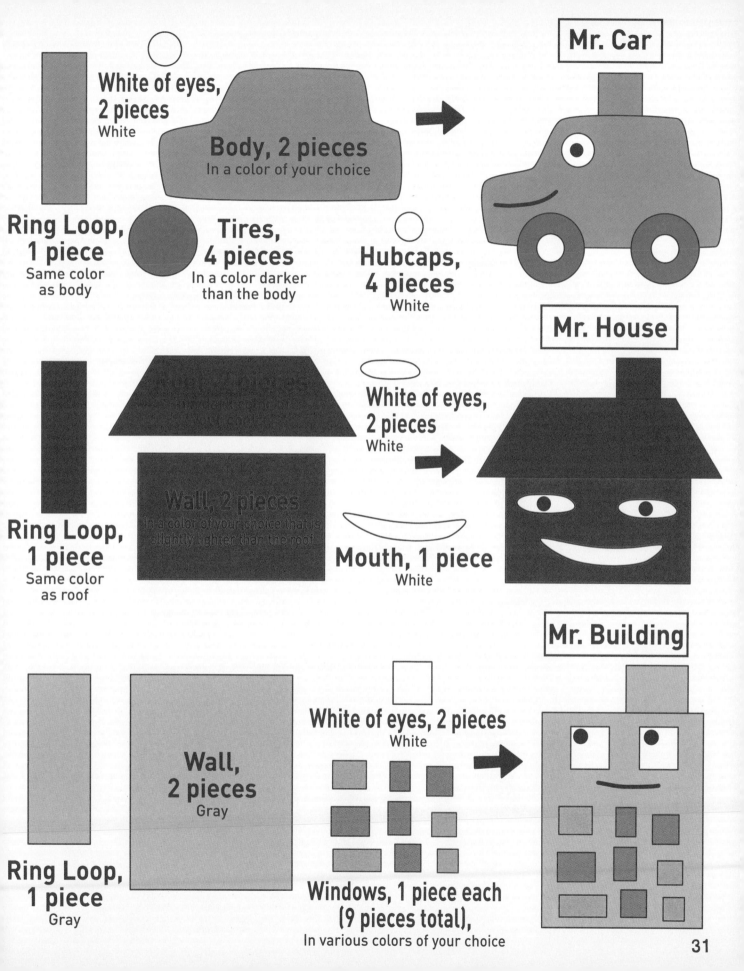

Mr. Car

White of eyes, 2 pieces
White

Body, 2 pieces
In a color of your choice

Ring Loop, 1 piece
Same color as body

Tires, 4 pieces
In a color darker than the body

Hubcaps, 4 pieces
White

Mr. House

Roof, 2 pieces
In a color of your choice

White of eyes, 2 pieces
White

Ring Loop, 1 piece
Same color as roof

Wall, 2 pieces
In a color of your choice that is slightly lighter than the roof

Mouth, 1 piece
White

Mr. Building

White of eyes, 2 pieces
White

Wall, 2 pieces
Gray

Ring Loop, 1 piece
Gray

Windows, 1 piece each (9 pieces total),
In various colors of your choice

31

The different colors of felt are very pretty.
Which colors do you like? Pick felt of colors you like.
Make matching coin cases and pouches.

How to Make Felt Coin Purses and Pouches

Here's how you make felt coin cases and felt pouches

`01`

Cut felt according to the respective patterns

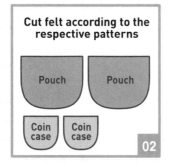

Pouch

Pouch

Coin case

Coin case

`02`

Cut felt for appliqué according to the pattern

If you want a Bad Guy appliqué

`03`

Make Bad Guy's face

Glue white of eyes and mouth

Make the pupils using an FN Stitch, turning 3 times (Black thread, 6 strands)

Glue lightly then cross-stitch

Black thread

`04`

Cut felt for appliqué according to the pattern

If you want a Panda appliqué

`05`

Make Panda's face

Glue eyes lightly, then cross-stitch

Make the nose using an FN Stitch, turning twice (Black thread, 6 strands)

Make the mouth using an S-Stitch (Black thread, 6 strands)

`06`

Decide position Insert ears and glue lightly

Cross-stitch

Black thread for ears
White thread for face

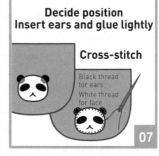

`07`

Cut felt for appliqué according to the pattern

If you want a White Rabbit appliqué

`08`

Make White Rabbit's face

Make the pupils using an FN Stitch, turning 3 times (Brown thread, 6 strands)

Make the nose using an FN Stitch, turning twice (Brown thread, 6 strands)

Make the mouth using an S-Stitch (Brown thread, 6 strands)

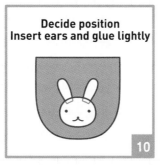

`09`

Decide position Insert ears and glue lightly

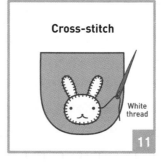

`10`

Cross-stitch

White thread

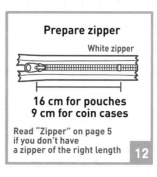

`11`

Prepare zipper

White zipper

**16 cm for pouches
9 cm for coin cases**

Read "Zipper" on page 5 if you don't have a zipper of the right length

`12`

Fold top 1 cm back towards reverse side

1 cm

Reverse

It'll be easier to sew if you iron the fold first

`13`

Keeping the top 1 cm folded, place on top of the zipper and tack

Sew about 0.5 cm in

Front

You can sew more neatly if you tack first

`14`

Sew about 0.3 cm in

Sew about 0.3 cm in with thread the same color as the felt

Front

Remove tacking thread after sewing

`15`

Sew the other side the same way

Front

Sew about 0.3 cm in after tacking

Thread same color as felt

Front

`16`

After attaching zipper, stack both halves inside out then sew along the dotted red line

Sew keeping the zipper half open

Reverse

Sew about 0.5 cm in

Thread same color as felt

`17`

Turn right side out through zipper opening

Reverse

`18`

Done

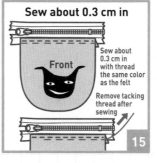

`19`

Matching felt bags on page 36!

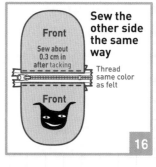

`20`

33

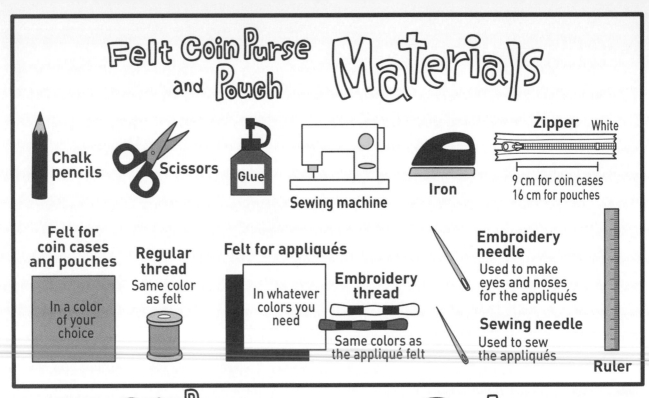

Felt Coin Purse and Pouch Materials

Chalk pencils

Scissors

Glue

Sewing machine

Iron

Zipper White
9 cm for coin cases
16 cm for pouches

Felt for coin cases and pouches
In a color of your choice

Regular thread
Same color as felt

Felt for appliqués
In whatever colors you need

Embroidery thread
Same colors as the appliqué felt

Embroidery needle
Used to make eyes and noses for the appliqués

Sewing needle
Used to sew the appliqués

Ruler

Felt Coin Purse and Pouch Appliqué Patterns

Patterns at 100% so no need to enlarge when copyir

Ears, 2 pieces
Black felt

Eyes, 2 pieces
Black felt

Face, 1 piece
White felt

Ears, 2 pieces
White felt

Face, 1 piece
White felt

Right white of eye, 1 piece
White felt

Left white of ey
White felt

Mouth, 1 piece
White felt

Face, 1 piece
Black felt

Felt Coin Purse and Pouch Patterns

Patterns at 100% so no need to enlarge when copying

Felt coin case, 2 pieces
Felt in color of your choice

Felt pouch, 2 pieces
Felt in color of your choice

Felt bags will look warm
if you carry them around in the winter.
But they'll look a little hot
if you carry them around in the summer.
You should probably forget about
carrying them around in the summer.

How to Make Felt Bags

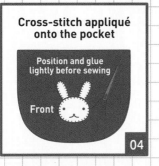

01
Here's how you make felt bags

02
Cut felt according to the felt bag patterns

Pocket, 1 piece
Bag, 2 pieces
Handle 2 pieces

03
Also cut felt for appliqué according to the pattern
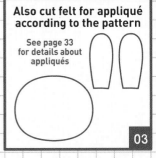
See page 33 for details about appliqués

04
Cross-stitch appliqué onto the pocket
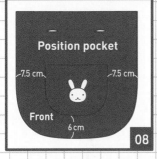
Position and glue lightly before sewing
Front

05
Draw a line 5 cm from the top of the bag on the reverse side
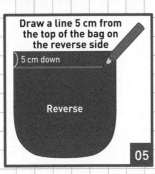
5 cm down
Reverse

06
Mark bag like so

3 cm 3 cm
8 cm 8 cm
Reverse

07
Cut slots along the portions indicated by the white lines

Reverse

08
Position pocket
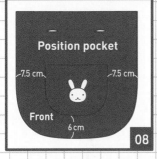
7.5 cm 7.5 cm
Front
6 cm

09
Tack about 0.8 cm in

About 0.8 cm in
You can sew more neatly if you tack first

10
Sew along the dotted white line, about 0.3 cm in
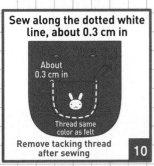
About 0.3 cm in
Thread same color as felt
Remove tacking thread after sewing

11
Stack halves of bag inside out and sew along the dotted white line

Sew 0.5 cm in
Turn right side out
Reverse

12
Fold at line after turning right side out

Front
It will come out neater if you iron along the fold

13
Make Handles It will come out neater if you iron along the fold!
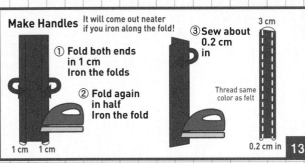
① Fold both ends in 1 cm Iron the folds
② Fold again in half Iron the fold
③ Sew about 0.2 cm in
3 cm
Thread same color as felt
1 cm 1 cm
0.2 cm in

14
Insert handles into the slots you cut out

Enough so that you can just see the ends of the handle
Front
Be careful not to twist the handles!

15
Sew along the dotted white line, about 1 cm from the top

1 cm down
Thread same color as felt
Front

16
Unfold the folded part at the top
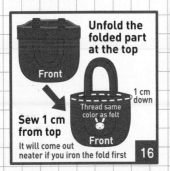
Front
1 cm down
Thread same color as felt
Front
Sew 1 cm from top
It will come out neater if you iron the fold first

17

Front
Make a smooth curve
Smooth out the shape and iron

18

Done

19

Make the matching coin cases and pouches on page 32!

37

Felt Bag Materials

 Chalk pencils

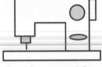 **Glue**

 Scissors

 **Ruler**

 **Iron**

Sewing machine

Felt in color of your choice

You can make the felt bag along with the felt coin case and pouch on page 32 if you have 3 pieces of 40 cm x 40 cm felt

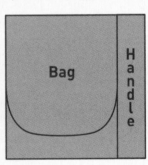

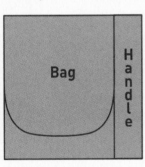

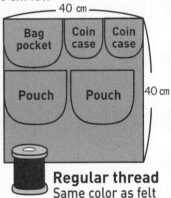

Regular thread
Same color as felt

Felt for appliqués
In the colors needed for the appliqués

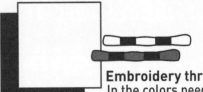

Embroidery thread
In the colors needed for the appliqués

Embroidery needle
Used to make eyes and noses for the appliqué

Sewing needle
Used to sew pockets of the appliqué

See page 33 for patterns and instructions on making appliqués

8 cm

Felt bag handle, 2 pieces
Felt in color of your choice

40 cm

Felt Bag Patterns

Enlarge to 180% for the ideal size
(You can also make the pattern by using a ruler instead of enlarging)

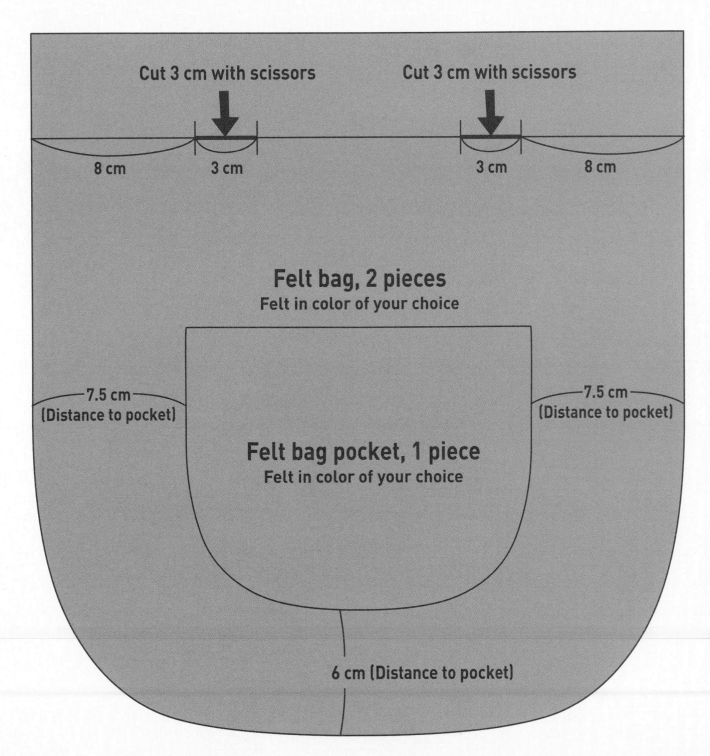

Cut 3 cm with scissors   Cut 3 cm with scissors

8 cm   3 cm   3 cm   8 cm

Felt bag, 2 pieces
Felt in color of your choice

7.5 cm
(Distance to pocket)   7.5 cm
(Distance to pocket)

Felt bag pocket, 1 piece
Felt in color of your choice

6 cm (Distance to pocket)

You can have your tissue cases make all sorts of faces.
You can twist up the mouth, open it wide, or have just a little tissue sticking out.
Let's make all sorts of fun faces.

How to Make Fun Tissue Cases

Cut fabric according to the pattern

`01`

Sew edges of the fabric with a zig-zag machine or an overlock machine

Prevent the fabric from fraying

`02`

Draw folding lines on reverse side of fabric

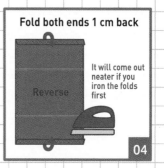

7 cm — Folding line A

10 cm — Reverse

6.5 cm — Folding line B

`03`

Fold both ends 1 cm back

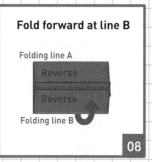

Reverse

It will come out neater if you iron the folds first

`04`

Sew along the dotted red line

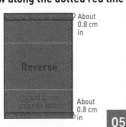

About 0.8 cm in

Reverse

Thread same color as fabric

About 0.8 cm in

`05`

Face up

Front

`06`

Fold forward at line A

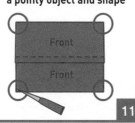

Folding line A

Reverse

Front

`07`

Fold forward at line B

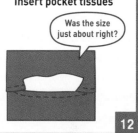

Folding line A

Reverse

Reverse

Folding line B

`08`

Sew along the dotted red line

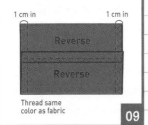

1 cm in   1 cm in

Reverse

Reverse

Thread same color as fabric

`09`

Turn right side out

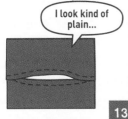

Reverse

Reverse

`10`

Neatly turn ends out using a pointy object and shape

Front

Front

`11`

Insert pocket tissues

Was the size just about right?

`12`

Do something to spruce them up

I look kind of plain...

`13`

**Cut felt according to the patterns
Position eyes and glue lightly
Cross-stitch**

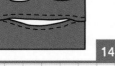

`14`

**Cut felt according to the patterns
Position eyes and glue lightly
Cross-stitch**

`15`

**Cut felt according to the patterns
Position eyes and drool and glue lightly
Cross-stitch**

`16`

Gimme some tissues.

If you have a Mr. Face tissue case...

`17`

Wow!

Here.

`18`

Super funny! Respect.

I just found it somewhere.

Actually, Liar worked very hard to make it

You could become very popular

`19`

If you don't want to make funny tissue cases, make pretty ones using printed fabrics and appliqués from pages 51 and 72.

`20`

FunTissue Case Materials

Chalk pencils

Scissors

Glue

Sewing machine

Overlock machine   If you have one

Iron

Ruler

Fabric
In a color of your choice
In a material of your choice

Regular thread
Same color as fabric

Felt
White   Black

Regular thread
White   Black

Sewing needle

Awl or other pointy object
Handy for turning out corners

FunTissue Case Patterns

Patterns at 100% so no need to enlarge when copying

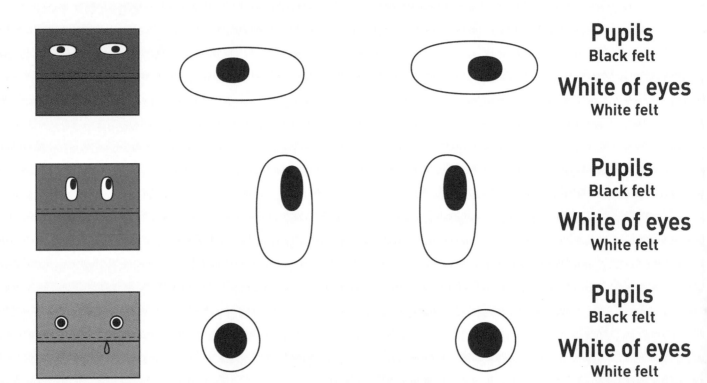

Pupils
Black felt

White of eyes
White felt

Pupils
Black felt

White of eyes
White felt

Pupils
Black felt

White of eyes
White felt

Drool
White felt

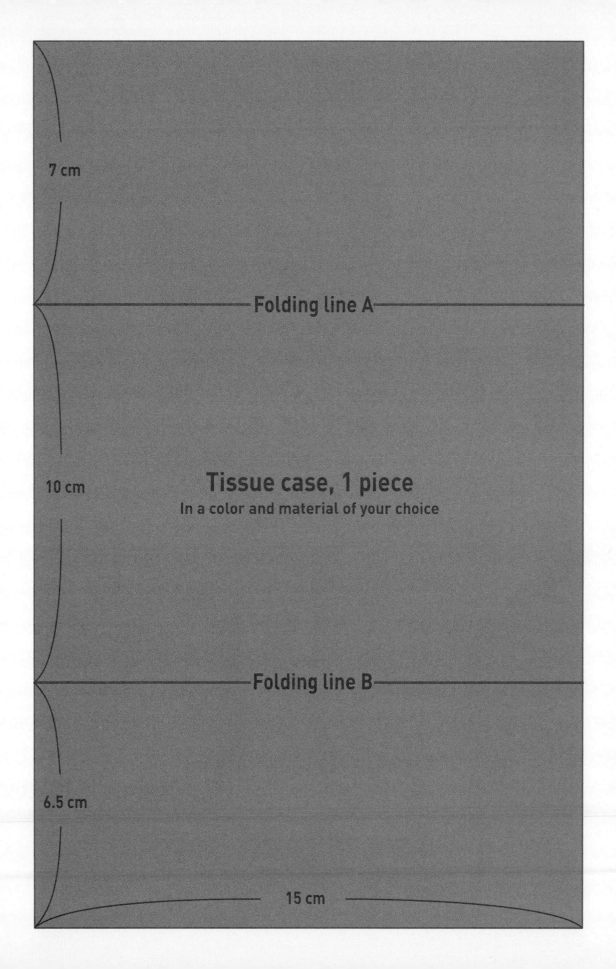

7 cm

Folding line A

10 cm

Tissue case, 1 piece
In a color and material of your choice

Folding line B

6.5 cm

15 cm

Easy Embroidery is easy to make.
It's easy, but you'll be surprised at how cute it is when you're done.
Just give it a shot. You really will be surprised at how cute it comes out.

How to Make Easy Embroidery

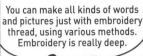 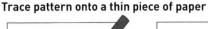 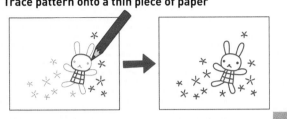

01
You can make all kinds of words and pictures just with embroidery thread, using various methods. Embroidery is really deep.

02
I'd like to explain some easy methods: not so much embroidery as making simple pictures with embroidery thread.

03
Trace pattern onto a thin piece of paper

04
Decide where you want to position your embroidery
Overlap in order from bottom to top

← Fabric you will embroider

Chalk paper
Pattern will be copied onto fabric as you trace over the chalk paper

← Thin paper with pattern

05
Trace pattern onto fabric

It should transfer without having to press too hard
It may come out too thick or the paper might rip if you press too hard

06
Blind stitch along traced lines (Embroidery thread, 3 strands)

Thread in color of your choice

Sew stitches as closely together as possible

Don't pull too hard or the fabric will wrinkle

07
No particular order
For nearby sections, span the distance under the fabric and keep sewing with the same thread

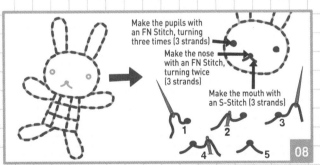

08
Make the pupils with an FN Stitch, turning three times (3 strands)

Make the nose with an FN Stitch, turning twice (3 strands)

Make the mouth with an S-Stitch (3 strands)

1 2 3
4 5

09
FN Stitch, turning twice (3 strands)

S-Stitch (3 strands)
S-Stitch for short lines

1 2

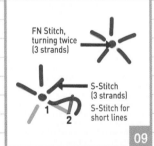

10

Done

11
Here's a summary of the instructions for Easy Embroidery:

Do close blind stitches for long lines and curves →

Do S-Stitches for short lines →

● Do an FN Stitch, turning once, for small circles
● Do an FN Stitch, turning twice, for medium circles
● Do an FN Stitch, turning three times, for large circles →

Try words and pictures not found in this book too!

12
Your plain handkerchiefs will become fabulous with Easy Embroidery

13

Make lunchbox wrappers with the right pictures on cloth napkins

Easy Embroidery Materials

 Scissors

Embroidery needle

Thin piece of paper
To trace patterns

Chalk paper for fabric
Used to trace pattern onto fabric

Fabric to embroider

In a material of your choice, such as a plain handkerchief or cloth napkin

Embroidery thread
In a color of your choice

Easy Embroidery Designs

Designs are at 100%, but you can enlarge or reduce as you wish

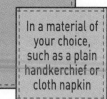

Mr. Drool Cup
Pupils: FN Stitch,
turning 3 times (6 strands)

If no sewing instructions are given, use a blind stitch (3 strands)

White Rabbit Flowers
Pupils: FN Stitch, turning 3 times (3 strands)
Nose: FN Stitch, turning twice (3 strands)
Mouth: S-Stitch (3 strands)
Lines for flowers: S-Stitch (3 strands)
Circles for flowers: FN Stitch, turning twice (3 strands)

Panda Spiral
Nose: FN Stitch, turning twice (3 strands)
Mouth: S-Stitch (3 strands)

Mr. Knife and Mr. Fork
Pupils: FN Stitch,
turning 3 times (3 strands)

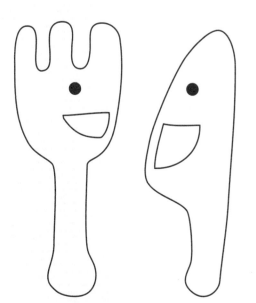

Bad Guy Aura
Pupils: FN Stitch,
turning 3 times (3 strands)

Sprite
Pupils: FN Stitch,
turning 3 times (3 strands)
Nose: FN Stitch,
turning once (3 strands)

Imagine you're exchanging name cards with a capable-looking young lady
in a business suit. What if she took her card out of a handmade card holder?
Wouldn't that be surprising? Wouldn't that be astonishing? Wouldn't that be fun?

white

How to Make Card Holders

Cut felt in a color of your choice according to the patterns

 Pattern A
 Pattern B
 Pattern D
Pattern C

01

You can sew the card holder with a machine or do a blind stitch by hand

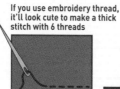

If you use embroidery thread, it'll look cute to make a thick stitch with 6 threads

Either is fine

02

Place Pattern C above Pattern B
Sew along the dotted red lines with thread in a color of your choice

Pattern C
Pattern B

Line up bottoms and sides before sewing

Side →
Sew about 0.3 cm in

↑ Bottom

03

Place Patterns B and C on top of Pattern A, tack, then sew along the dotted red line

 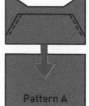

Pattern A

Tack before sewing so pieces stay aligned

Remove tacking thread after sewing

Sew about 0.3 cm in

Line up bottoms and sides before sewing

04

Place Pattern D on top
Sew along the dotted red line

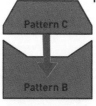
Pattern D

Top
Side →
Sew about 0.3 cm in

Line up tops and sides before sewing

05

 Front

 Put cards in

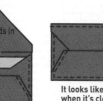

Back

Done

It looks like this when it's open

It looks like this when it's closed
The cards won't fall out

06

A cardholder would look cute with appliqués stitched on. Take care to make small, high-quality appliqués.

You can do the appliqués before or after you sew the card holder together

If you want to apply them somewhere that will be hard to reach after sewing, do them before sewing

07

Cut felt as indicated in the appliqué patterns

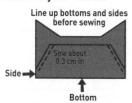

Cut as many as you want in colors of your choice

08

Position appliqués

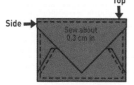

Glue

09

FN Stitch in the center of the flower

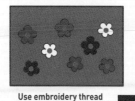

Use embroidery thread in a color of your choice

10

Front

Back

Done

11

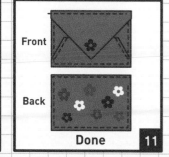  

Isn't it cute?
You can put business cards and health insurance cards and discount cards inside.

Try to make a card holder as cute as the one White Rabbit made, and then use it every day!

12

Card Holder Materials

Chalk pencils

Scissors

Glue

Embroidery needle
Used for FN Stitches and S-Stitches
Also used to sew card holders with embroidery thread

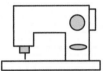
Sewing machine

Felt
In a color of your choice

Regular thread
In a color of your choice

Embroidery thread
In a color of your choice

Card Holder Patterns

Patterns at 100% so no need to enlarge when copying

Pattern A, 1 piece
Felt in a color of your choice

Pattern B, 1 piece
Felt in a color of your choice

Pattern D, 1 piece
Felt in a color of your choice

Pattern C, 1 piece
Felt in a color of your choice

Card Holder Appliqué Patterns

Patterns at 100% so no need to enlarge when copying
Use felt and embroidery thread in colors of your choice

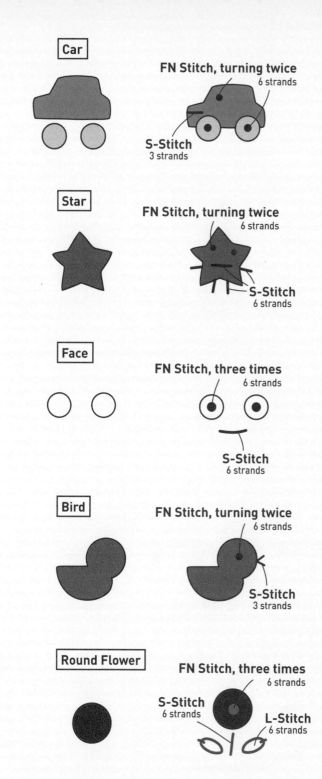

Car

FN Stitch, turning twice
6 strands

S-Stitch
3 strands

Star

FN Stitch, turning twice
6 strands

S-Stitch
6 strands

Face

FN Stitch, three times
6 strands

S-Stitch
6 strands

Bird

FN Stitch, turning twice
6 strands

S-Stitch
3 strands

Round Flower

FN Stitch, three times
6 strands

S-Stitch
6 strands

L-Stitch
6 strands

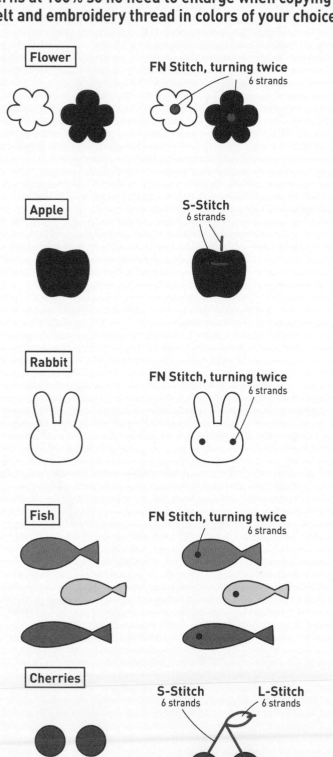

Flower

FN Stitch, turning twice
6 strands

Apple

S-Stitch
6 strands

Rabbit

FN Stitch, turning twice
6 strands

Fish

FN Stitch, turning twice
6 strands

Cherries

S-Stitch
6 strands

L-Stitch
6 strands

How to sew an L-Stitch (Lazy Daisy Stitch)

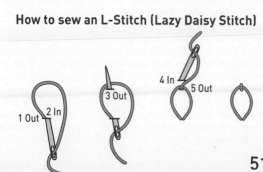

1 Out   2 In

3 Out

4 In   5 Out

Mr. Face is always smiling. He carries your heavy belongings with a smile, and goes with you everywhere with a smile. He smiles whether it's hot out or cold.

52

How to Make Mr. Face Bags

First, decide the length, width, and handle length of the bag you want

C Handle length

A Length

B Width

`01`

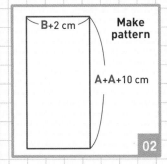

B+2 cm

Make pattern

A+A+10 cm

`02`

Trace pattern onto fabric and cut

`03`

Sew edges of the fabric with a zig-zag machine or an overlock machine (to prevent the fabric from fraying)

`04`

4 cm

Reverse

4 cm

Draw two lines 4 cm from the top and bottom

`05`

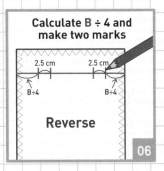

Calculate B ÷ 4 and make two marks

2.5 cm   2.5 cm

B÷4   B÷4

Reverse

`06`

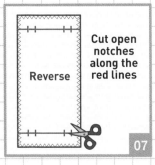

Reverse

Cut open notches along the red lines

`07`

Make patterns for eyes and mouth in whatever size you want, then cut fabric according to the patterns (fabric could be felt or some other fabric)

A color similar to the handle would be cute
A different color would also be cute

`08`

Fold forward in half and position eyes and mouth

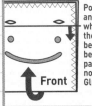

Front

Position eyes and mouth below where you cut the notches because you will be folding the part above the notches
Glue lightly

`09`

Cross-stitch eyes and mouth or use a zig-zag machine around the eyes and mouth

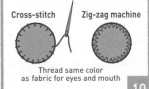

Cross-stitch   Zig-zag machine

Thread same color as fabric for eyes and mouth

`10`

Turn inside out and fold in two Sew 1 cm in on both ends

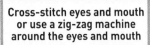

The slats you made will create two openings
Reverse

`11`

Turn right side out

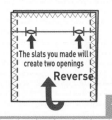

Reverse

Thread same color as fabric

`12`

Fold at line after turning right side out

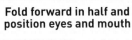

Front

It will come out neater if you iron the fold first

`13`

Cut two strips of 2.5 cm-wide tape

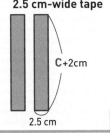

C+2cm

2.5 cm

`14`

Insert handles where you cut the notches

Far enough so you can just see the ends of the handles

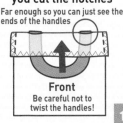

Front

Be careful not to twist the handles!

`15`

Sew along the circumference, 1 cm down

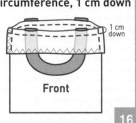

1 cm down

Front

`16`

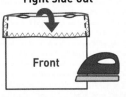

Front

Unfold the bag

Front

`17`

Sew along the circumference, 1 cm down

1 cm down

Front

It will come out neater if you iron the fold first

`18`

Done

`19`

Make Mr. Face bags in various shapes and colors!

`20`

53

Mr. Face Bag Materials

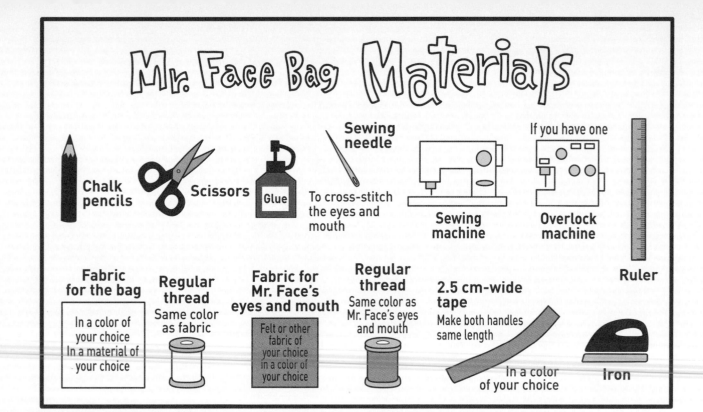

Chalk pencils

Scissors

Glue — To cross-stitch the eyes and mouth

Sewing needle

Sewing machine

Overlock machine — If you have one

Ruler

Fabric for the bag — In a color of your choice. In a material of your choice

Regular thread — Same color as fabric

Fabric for Mr. Face's eyes and mouth — Felt or other fabric of your choice in a color of your choice

Regular thread — Same color as Mr. Face's eyes and mouth

2.5 cm-wide tape — Make both handles same length. In a color of your choice

Iron

Mr. Face Bag Patterns

You can enlarge or reduce this pattern to exactly the size you want

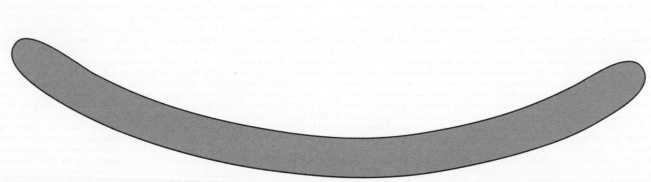

These are just sample sizes
If you want sizes other than these, read the instructions
on page 53 and make your own patterns
Try all sorts of sizes!

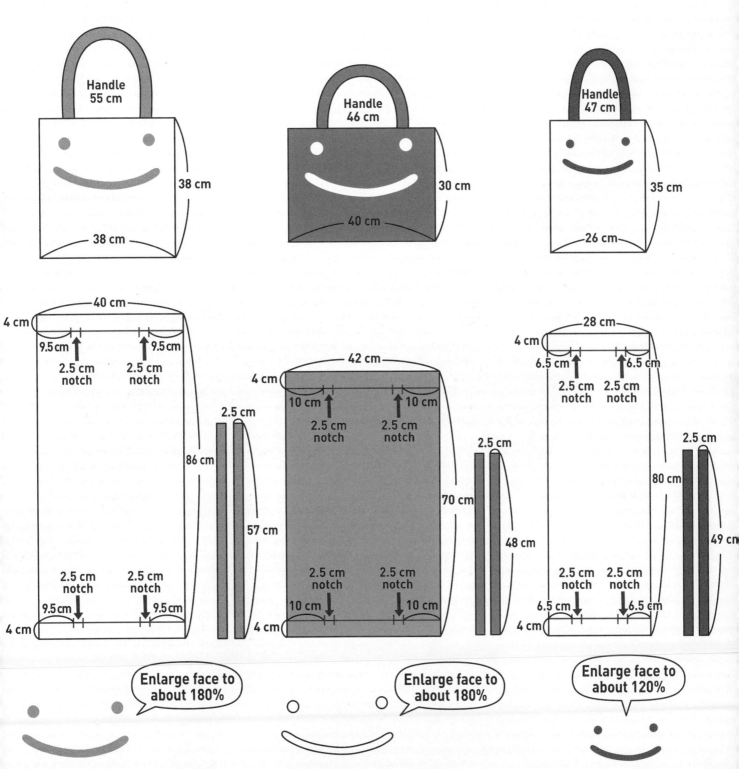

Handle 55 cm
38 cm
38 cm

Handle 46 cm
30 cm
40 cm

Handle 47 cm
35 cm
26 cm

40 cm
4 cm
9.5 cm 9.5 cm
2.5 cm notch 2.5 cm notch
2.5 cm
86 cm
57 cm
2.5 cm notch 2.5 cm notch
9.5 cm 9.5 cm
4 cm

42 cm
4 cm
10 cm 10 cm
2.5 cm notch 2.5 cm notch
2.5 cm
70 cm
48 cm
2.5 cm notch 2.5 cm notch
10 cm 10 cm
4 cm

28 cm
4 cm
6.5 cm 6.5 cm
2.5 cm notch 2.5 cm notch
2.5 cm
80 cm
49 cm
2.5 cm notch 2.5 cm notch
6.5 cm 6.5 cm
4 cm

Enlarge face to about 180%

Enlarge face to about 180%

Enlarge face to about 120%

55

It's hot! I'm thirsty! I'm gonna drink a lot!
I'm gonna drink all of these.
It's okay, because they'll stay cool in my
Mr. Sweaty plastic bottle holders.

How to Make Mr. Sweaty Bottle Holders

01 Isn't it a pain when the insides of your bags get wet because the cold plastic bottles you put inside sweat so much? Isn't it a pain when your cold drinks in plastic bottles get tepid and lukewarm? Isn't it a pain when your warm drinks cool down? A real pain!

02 Wow. Pretty good. I know! Let's put some clothes on these bottles. A plastic bottle holder. Let's make one!

03 Cut fabric according to the patterns

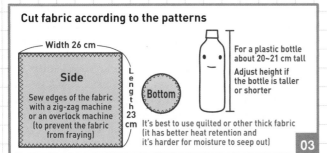

Width 26 cm

Side
Sew edges of the fabric with a zig-zag machine or an overlock machine (to prevent the fabric from fraying)

Length 23 cm

Bottom

For a plastic bottle about 20~21 cm tall

Adjust height if the bottle is taller or shorter

It's best to use quilted or other thick fabric (it has better heat retention and it's harder for moisture to seep out)

04 Cut felt according to the Mr. Sweaty patterns

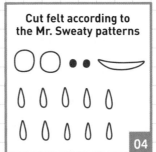

05 Position eyes and mouth

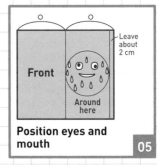

Leave about 2 cm

Front

Around here

06 Glue lightly before doing a cross-stitch

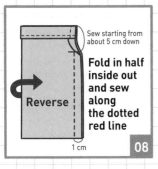

White thread for white of eyes — Brown thread for pupils

White thread for mouth

White thread for sweat

07

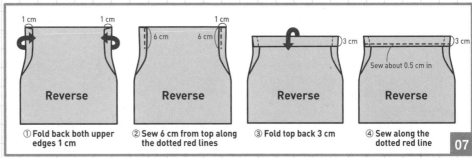

① Fold back both upper edges 1 cm
② Sew 6 cm from top along the dotted red lines
③ Fold top back 3 cm
④ Sew along the dotted red line (Sew about 0.5 cm in)

Reverse

08

Sew starting from about 5 cm down

Fold in half inside out and sew along the dotted red line

Reverse

1 cm

09

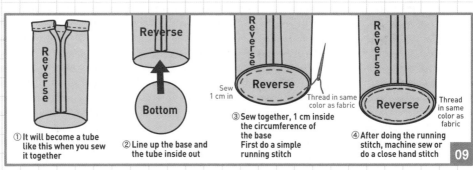

① It will become a tube like this when you sew it together
② Line up the base and the tube inside out
③ Sew together, 1 cm inside the circumference of the base. First do a simple running stitch (Sew 1 cm in — Thread in same color as fabric)
④ After doing the running stitch, machine sew or do a close hand stitch (Thread in same color as fabric)

Reverse / Bottom

10

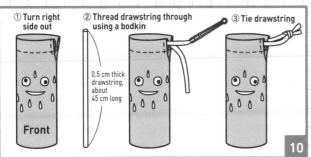

① Turn right side out
② Thread drawstring through using a bodkin (0.5 cm thick drawstring, about 45 cm long)
③ Tie drawstring

Front

11 Done

Make Mr. Sweaty in all sorts of different colors He'll work up a sweat working hard for you

Mr. Sweaty Bottle Holder Materials

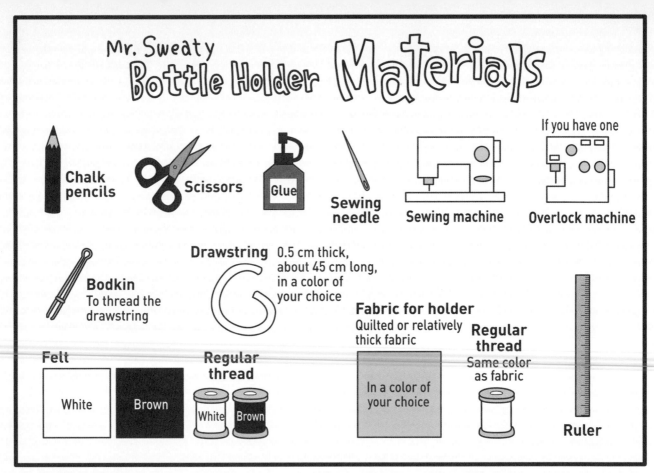

Chalk pencils

Scissors

Glue

Sewing needle

Sewing machine

If you have one

Overlock machine

Bodkin
To thread the drawstring

Drawstring 0.5 cm thick, about 45 cm long, in a color of your choice

Felt
White
Brown

Regular thread
White
Brown

Fabric for holder
Quilted or relatively thick fabric
In a color of your choice

Regular thread
Same color as fabric

Ruler

Mr. Sweaty Bottle Holder Appliqué Patterns

Patterns at 100% so no need to enlarge when copying

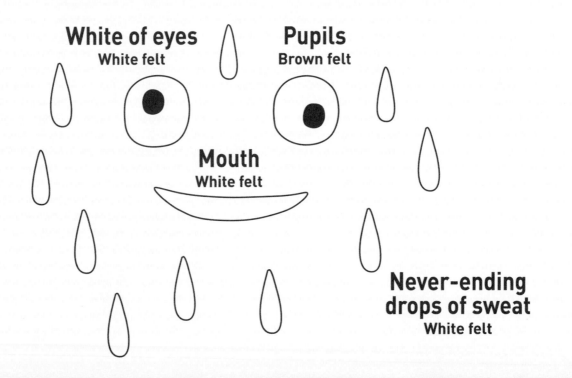

White of eyes
White felt

Pupils
Brown felt

Mouth
White felt

Never-ending drops of sweat
White felt

Mr. Sweaty
Bottle Holder Patterns

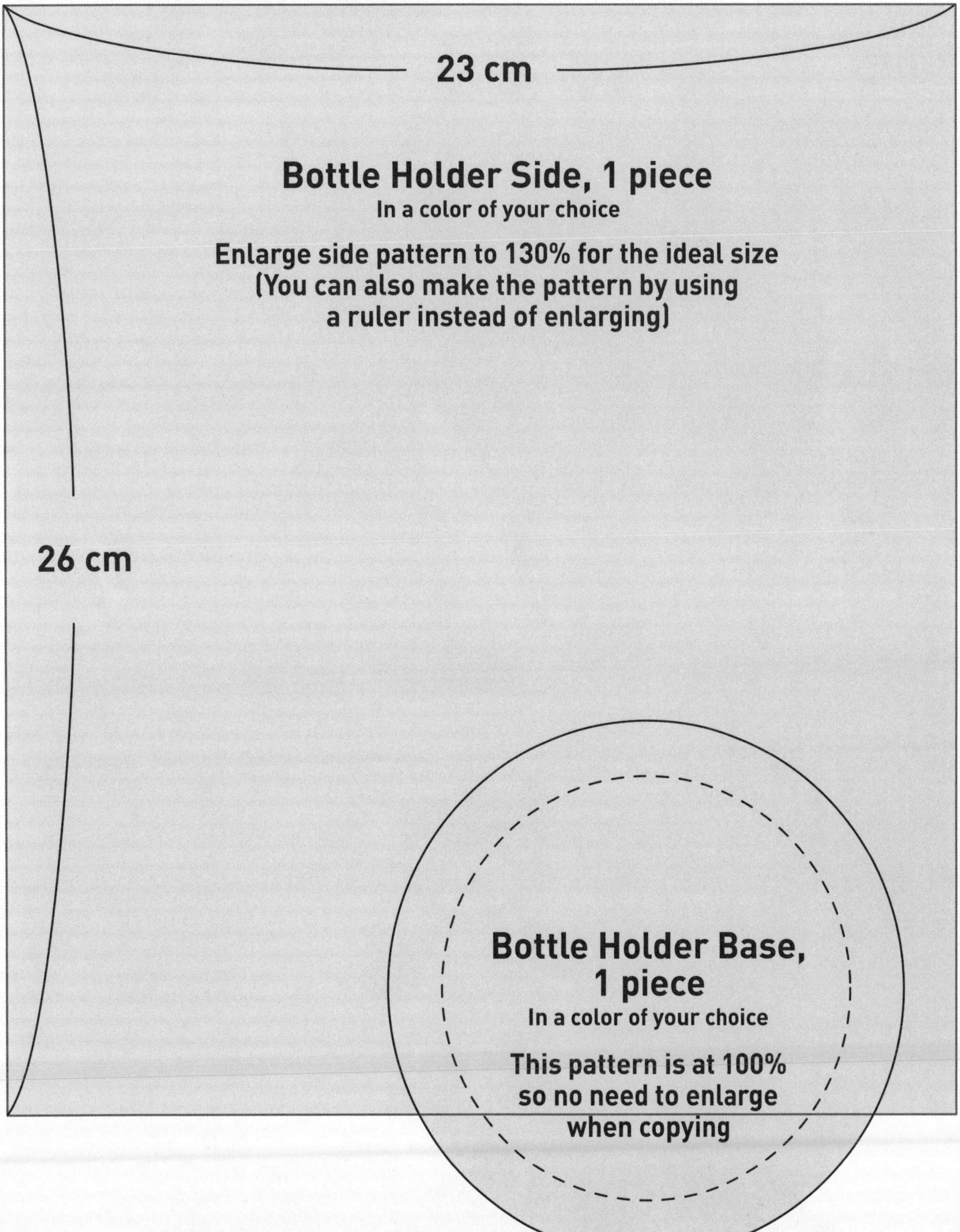

23 cm

Bottle Holder Side, 1 piece
In a color of your choice

**Enlarge side pattern to 130% for the ideal size
(You can also make the pattern by using
a ruler instead of enlarging)**

26 cm

Bottle Holder Base, 1 piece
In a color of your choice

**This pattern is at 100%
so no need to enlarge
when copying**

It isn't always easy trying to find a bag
in exactly the size you want.
At times like that, you just go ahead
and make a bag in exactly the size you want.
Yeah, let's just go ahead.

How to Make Gusseted Ecological Bags

01
Let's conserve our limited natural resources. Take an Ecological Bag with you when you go shopping.

02

The Gusseted Ecological Bag can hold a lot of stuff. Let's try making one. You can use any fabric you have around the house.

Take a look at Mr. Face Bag on page 53 for reference if you want to make a flat Ecological Bag

03
Decide how big you want your bag to be

D Handle length
A Length
B Width
C Width of gusset

04
Make patterns
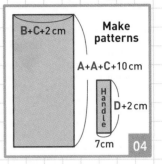
B+C+2 cm
A+A+C+10 cm
Handle
D+2 cm
7 cm

05
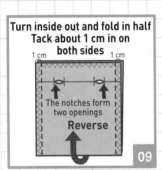
Bag
Handle Handle

Trace onto fabric and cut

Sew edges of the fabric with a zig-zag machine or an overlock machine (to prevent the fabric from fraying)

06
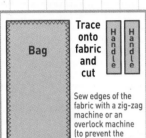
Reverse
4 cm
4 cm
Draw lines 4 cm inside on both ends

07
Calculate C ÷ 2 and B ÷ 4 and mark
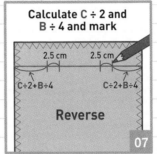
2.5 cm 2.5 cm
C÷2+B÷4   C÷2+B÷4
Reverse

08
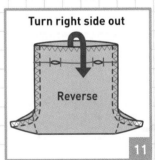
Reverse
Cut notches along the red lines

09
Turn inside out and fold in half Tack about 1 cm in on both sides
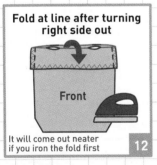
1 cm   1 cm
The notches form two openings
Reverse

10
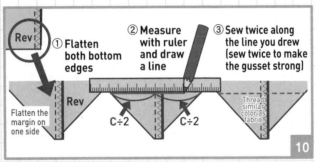
Rev
① Flatten both bottom edges
② Measure with ruler and draw a line
③ Sew twice along the line you drew (sew twice to make the gusset strong)
Flatten the margin on one side
Rev
C÷2   C÷2
Thread similar color as fabric

11
Turn right side out
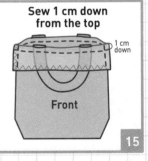
Reverse

12
Fold at line after turning right side out

Front
It will come out neater if you iron the fold first

13
Make Handles
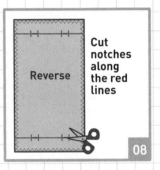
① Fold 1 cm on both ends
② Fold in two
③ Sew about 0.2 cm in along the dotted red lines
It will come out neater if you iron the fold first
2.5 cm

14
Insert handles into the notches

Just enough to see the edges of the handles
Front
Be careful not to twist the handles!

15
Sew 1 cm down from the top

1 cm down
Front

16

Unfold
Front
Front

17
Sew 1 cm from top all around

1 cm down
Front
It will come out neater if you iron the fold first

18

Appliqués would be cute, and printed fabrics would be nice
It's done!

19
Now I'm an Ecological Rabbit when I go shopping!

Gusseted Ecological Bag Materials

Chalk pencils

Scissors

Iron

Sewing machine

If you have one
Overlock machine

Ruler

Fabric for bag
In a color of your choice
In a material of your choice

Regular thread
Same color as fabric

These are some sample sizes for your Gusseted Ecological Bag.
If you want to make sizes other than these, read the instructions on page 61 and make your own patterns.
It's called an Ecological Bag, so of course you can use it for all sorts of things besides shopping.
Make bags of all different sizes!

Large bag

Handle 55 cm

A size you'll want to carry around every day because it can carry just about anything. You could even use it for an overnight trip.

33 cm

33 cm

Gusset 13 cm

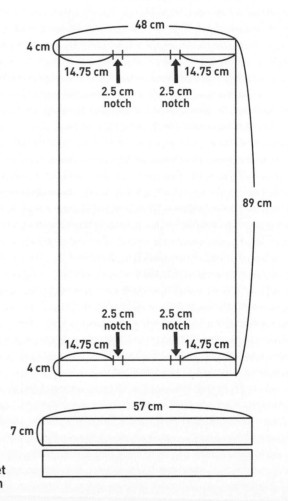

48 cm

4 cm

14.75 cm

2.5 cm notch

2.5 cm notch

14.75 cm

89 cm

2.5 cm notch

2.5 cm notch

14.75 cm

14.75 cm

4 cm

57 cm

7 cm

Very large bag

Handle 45 cm

This is a good size for some major shopping: daikon radishes, scallions, pumpkins, onions, potatoes and more

42 cm

Gusset 15 cm

32 cm

---

49 cm

4 cm

15.5 cm   15.5 cm

2.5 cm notch   2.5 cm notch

109 cm

2.5 cm notch   2.5 cm notch

15.5 cm   15.5 cm

4 cm

---

47 cm

7 cm

Medium bag

Handle 30 cm

Great as a second bag for when you're commuting to work or school

34 cm

Gusset 9 cm

28 cm

---

39 cm

4 cm

11.5 cm   11.5 cm

2.5 cm notch   2.5 cm notch

87 cm

2.5 cm notch   2.5 cm notch

11.5 cm   11.5 cm

4 cm

---

32 cm

7 cm

Small bag

Handle 27 cm

21 cm

A perfect size to hold a lunch box

Gusset 12 cm

21 cm

---

35 cm

4 cm

11.25 cm   11.25 cm

2.5 cm notch   2.5 cm notch

64 cm

2.5 cm notch   2.5 cm notch

11.25 cm   11.25 cm

4 cm

---

29 cm

7 cm

"Your gecko's so cool."
"Your ladybug is awesome."
"Can I have that frog?"
"Gimme that turtle."
That's what the boys at school will say.
You might become really popular among them.

64

How To Make Ladybug

Cut felt according to the patterns

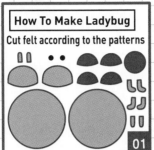

`01`

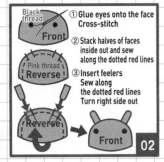

Black thread
Front

① Glue eyes onto the face Cross-stitch

Pink thread
Reverse

② Stack halves of faces inside out and sew along the dotted red lines

Reverse

③ Insert feelers Sew along the dotted red lines Turn right side out

Front

`02`

Glue spots lightly and cross-stitch

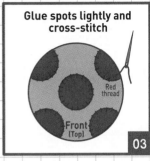

Red thread

Front (Top)

`03`

Make a hole for the zipper in the middle of the other half of the body

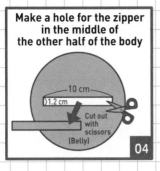

10 cm
1.2 cm
Cut out with scissors
(Belly)

`04`

Sew zipper

Light pink zipper

9 cm

Prepare by reading "Zipper" on page 5

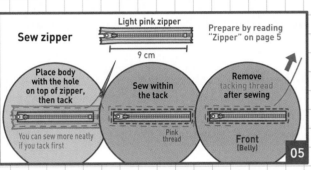

Place body with the hole on top of zipper, then tack

You can sew more neatly if you tack first

Sew within the tack

Pink thread

Remove tacking thread after sewing

Front (Belly)

`05`

① Place face and legs on top of body (top) Sew along the dotted blue lines

Pink thread
Front (Top)

Place the face folded back with the eyes facing down

② Stack halves of bodies inside out and sew along the dotted red line

Reverse (Belly)

Pink thread

Keep zipper in belly open

③ Turn right side out through the zipper opening

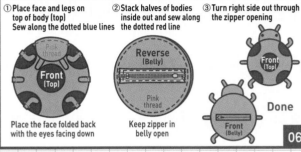

Front (Top)

Front (Belly)

Done

`06`

How To Make Turtle

Cut felt according to the patterns

`01`

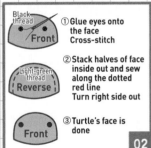

Black thread
Front

① Glue eyes onto the face Cross-stitch

Light-green thread
Reverse

② Stack halves of face inside out and sew along the dotted red line Turn right side out

Front

③ Turtle's face is done

`02`

Green zipper

9 cm

Make a hole for the zipper in the middle of the body

10 cm
1.2 cm
(Belly)

Green thread

Front (Belly)

Place body on top of zipper and sew along the dotted red line

`03`

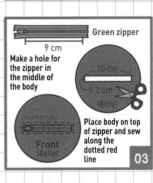

Green thread
Front (Shell)

① Place face, legs, and tail on top of body (shell) Sew along the dotted red line Place the face folded back with the eyes facing down

② Stack halves of bodies inside out and sew along the dotted red line

③ Turn right side out through the zipper

Green thread
Back (Belly)

Front (Shell)   **Front** (Belly)

Done

`04`

How To Make Frog

Cut felt according to the patterns

`01`

Glue eyes and stripes lightly onto the body Cross-stitch

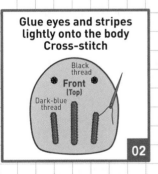

Black thread
Front (Top)

Dark-blue thread

`02`

Light-blue zipper

9 cm

Make a hole for the zipper in the middle of the other half of the body

10 cm
1.2 cm
(Belly)

Light-blue thread

Front (Belly)

Place body on top of zipper and sew along the dotted red line

`03`

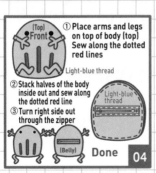

(Top)
Front

① Place arms and legs on top of body (top) Sew along the dotted red lines

Light-blue thread

② Stack halves of the body inside out and sew along the dotted red line

③ Turn right side out through the zipper

Light-blue thread
(Belly)

Done

`04`

How To Make Gecko

Cut felt according to the patterns

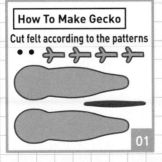

`01`

Glue eyes and stripe lightly onto the body Cross-stitch

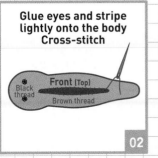

Black thread
Front (Top)
Brown thread

`02`

Brown zipper

15 cm

Make a hole for the zipper in the middle of the other half of the body

16 cm
1.2 cm   (Belly)

Place body on top of zipper and sew along the dotted red line

Brown thread
Front   (Belly)

`03`

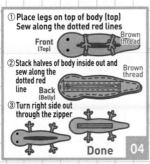

① Place legs on top of body (top) Sew along the dotted red lines

Front (Top)
Brown thread

② Stack halves of body inside out and sew along the dotted red line

Brown thread
Back (Belly)

③ Turn right side out through the zipper

Done

`04`

Bug Materials

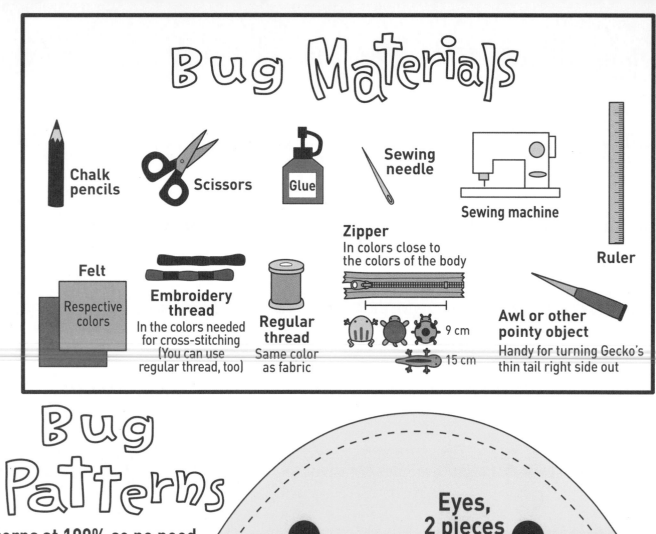

Chalk pencils

Scissors

Glue

Sewing needle

Sewing machine

Ruler

Felt
Respective colors

Embroidery thread
In the colors needed for cross-stitching (You can use regular thread, too)

Regular thread
Same color as fabric

Zipper
In colors close to the colors of the body

9 cm

15 cm

Awl or other pointy object
Handy for turning Gecko's thin tail right side out

Bug Patterns

Patterns at 100% so no need to enlarge when copying

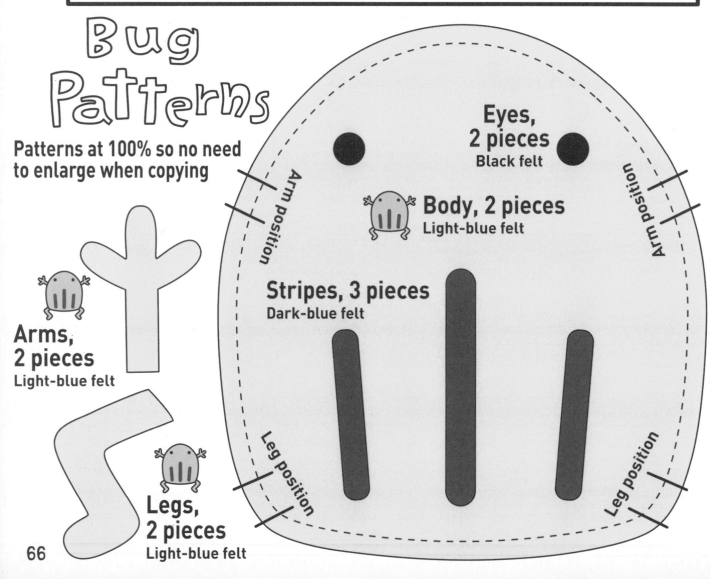

Arms, 2 pieces
Light-blue felt

Legs, 2 pieces
Light-blue felt

Eyes, 2 pieces
Black felt

Body, 2 pieces
Light-blue felt

Stripes, 3 pieces
Dark-blue felt

Arm position

Arm position

Leg position

Leg position

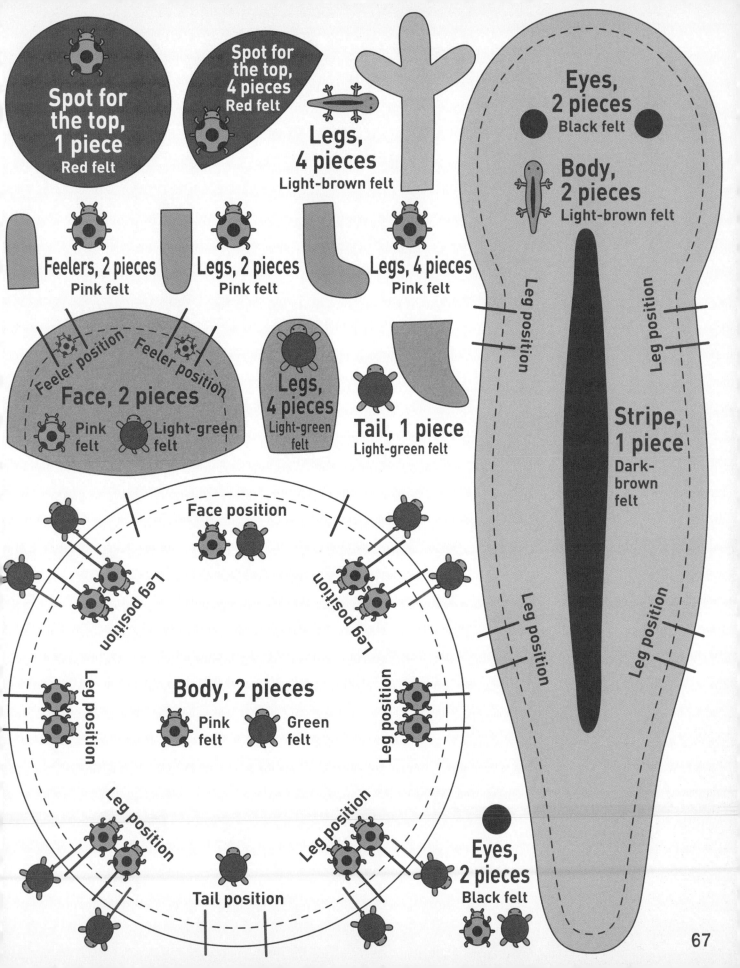

Spot for the top, 1 piece
Red felt

Spot for the top, 4 pieces
Red felt

Legs, 4 pieces
Light-brown felt

Feelers, 2 pieces
Pink felt

Legs, 2 pieces
Pink felt

Legs, 4 pieces
Pink felt

Feeler position   Feeler position

Face, 2 pieces
Pink felt   Light-green felt

Legs, 4 pieces
Light-green felt

Tail, 1 piece
Light-green felt

Eyes, 2 pieces
Black felt

Body, 2 pieces
Light-brown felt

Leg position   Leg position

Stripe, 1 piece
Dark-brown felt

Leg position   Leg position

Face position

Leg position   Leg position

Leg position   Leg position

Body, 2 pieces
Pink felt   Green felt

Leg position   Leg position

Tail position

Eyes, 2 pieces
Black felt

Don't make fun of them just because their bodies are long.
Sometimes it helps to have a long body.
They'll wrap around your neck and keep you warm.
If your neck is warm, your whole body stays warm.

How to Make Long Doll Scarves

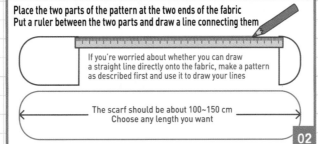

Copy the body pattern and cut into two at the Length Adjustment Line

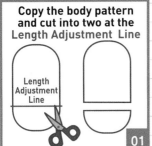

Length Adjustment Line

01

Place the two parts of the pattern at the two ends of the fabric
Put a ruler between the two parts and draw a line connecting them

If you're worried about whether you can draw a straight line directly onto the fabric, make a pattern as described first and use it to draw your lines

The scarf should be about 100~150 cm
Choose any length you want

02

Cut fabric and felt according to the patterns

03

Cut fabric and felt according to the patterns

04

Cut fabric and felt according to the patterns

05

Position eyes, nose, and mouth
Glue lightly before doing a cross-stitch

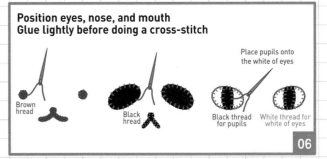

Brown thread

Black thread

Place pupils onto the white of eyes

Black thread for pupils

White thread for white of eyes

06

Stack halves of arms, legs, and ears inside out and sew along the dotted red lines

Thread same color as body

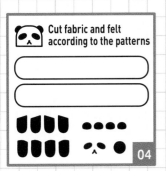

Reverse — Arm

Reverse — Leg

Reverse — Ear

07

Turn right side out

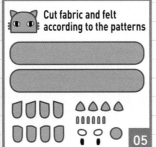

Reverse / Reverse

Reverse

Front / Front

Front

08

Stack halves of bodies inside out and sew only along the dotted red lines

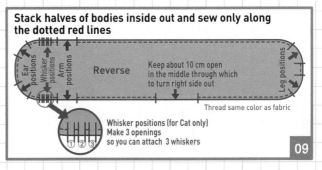

Ear positions / Whisker positions / Arm positions

Reverse

Keep about 10 cm open in the middle through which to turn right side out

Leg positions

Thread same color as fabric

Whisker positions (for Cat only)
Make 3 openings so you can attach 3 whiskers

① ② ③

09

Insert arms, legs, ears, and (for Cat only) whiskers between the two stacked halves of the body
Sew along the dotted red lines

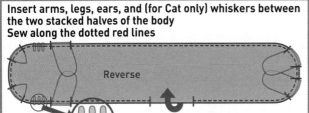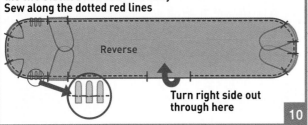

Reverse

Turn right side out through here

10

Sew the opening shut after turning right side out

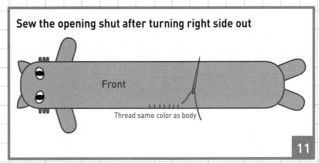

Front

Thread same color as body

11

Sew along the dotted red line

It's a tail, meow.

Cotton

Thread same color as fabric

Stuff cotton and pull the thread, making a ball

Tight

12

Sew tail onto the body (at the backside)

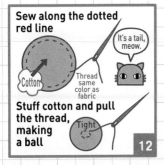

Thread same color as body

13

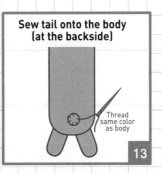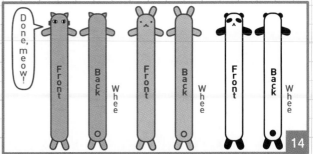

Done, meow!

Front / Back / Whee

Front / Back / Whee

Front / Back / Whee

14

Long Doll Scarf Materials

Chalk pencils

Scissors

Glue

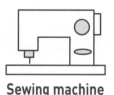
Sewing machine

Cotton

Ruler

Fabric for scarf
For winter, we recommend warm materials like fleece
You can use cotton for spring and fall
Use any color you like

Thread
Use stretch thread for stretchable fabrics

Felt
In respective colors

Regular thread
In the colors needed for cross-stitching the felt

Sewing needle

Ears, 4 pieces
In a color of your choice
In a fabric of your choice

Ears, 4 pieces
Black, in the fabric of your choice

Eyes, 2 pieces
Black felt

Ears, 4 pieces
In a color of your choice
In a fabric of your choice

Whiskers, 6 pieces
Felt in a color of your choice

Eyes, 2 pieces
Brown felt

Nose and mouth, 1 piece
Black felt

Right white of eye, 1 piece
White felt

Black felt
Right pupil, 1 piece

Nose and mouth, 1 piece
Brown felt

Left white of eye, 1 piece
White felt

Black felt
Left pupil, 1 piece

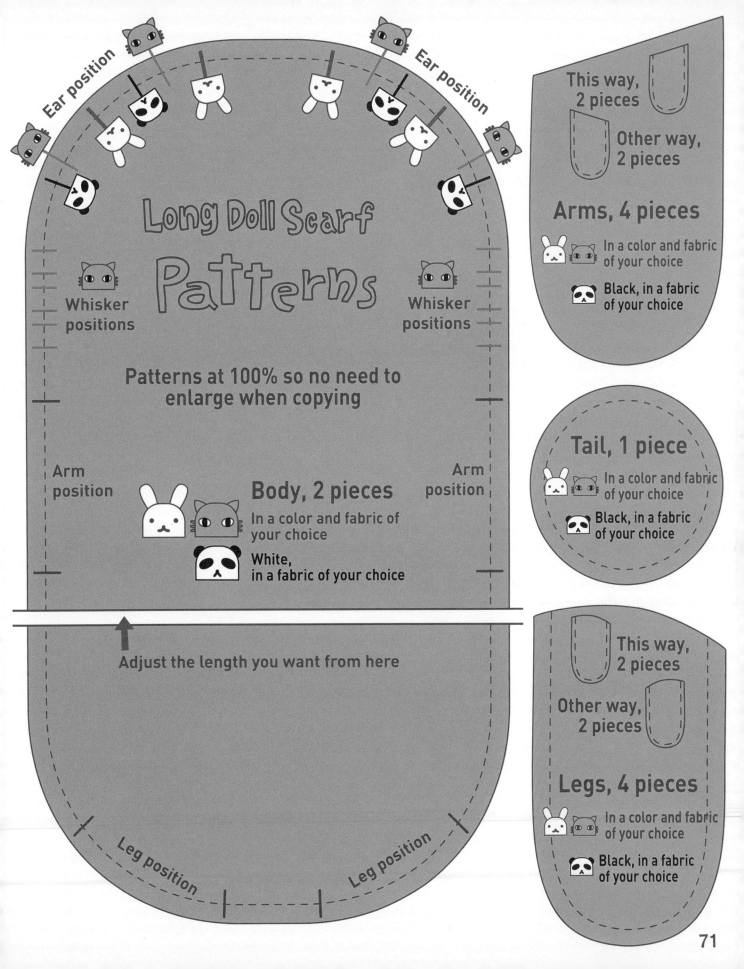

Long Doll Scarf Patterns

Ear position

Ear position

Whisker positions

Whisker positions

Patterns at 100% so no need to enlarge when copying

Arm position

Arm position

Body, 2 pieces

In a color and fabric of your choice

White, in a fabric of your choice

Adjust the length you want from here

Leg position

Leg position

This way, 2 pieces

Other way, 2 pieces

Arms, 4 pieces

In a color and fabric of your choice

Black, in a fabric of your choice

Tail, 1 piece

In a color and fabric of your choice

Black, in a fabric of your choice

This way, 2 pieces

Other way, 2 pieces

Legs, 4 pieces

In a color and fabric of your choice

Black, in a fabric of your choice

Appliqués are cute. Appliqués are easy. Appliqués are fun.
Appliqués are good. Let's make some appliqués.

How to Make Fun Appliqués

01 Some pretty good things can happen when you make appliqués.

02 This bag looks kind of dreary...  but look how cute it is when you add appliqués!

03 If you pick a personal logo and make appliqués of it...  you can easily identify your own things

04 If you carry around things you've appliquéd...
Wow, I'm so jealous! I want one too! What? You made it? Wow, you're a genius!
people get jealous of you and treat you like a genius

05 First make your pattern. You can just copy the patterns on a Pattern page, or enlarge or reduce them to the sizes you want.

06 Cut felt as indicated in the patterns  The colors for the felt and embroidery thread for stitching indicated in the Patterns pages are just suggestions You can use whatever color you like for the felt and thread

07 Look at the finished version (marked "Done!") and position the felt in order: 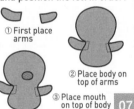 ① First place arms ② Place body on top of arms ③ Place mouth on top of body

08 Glue after positioning  Glue

09 Cross-stitch edges of felt 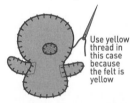 Use yellow thread in this case because the felt is yellow
Try to use thread of the same color as the felt

10 Make pupils, nose, lips, and legs with embroidery thread  Pupils: FN Stitch, turning 3 times
Lips: S-Stitch
Legs: S-Stitch
Done!

11 If you think that this all sounds too difficult and troublesome, here are two simple appliqué methods as alternatives:
Glue firmly  Draw
Glue
Simple Method 1 You don't have to cross-stitch if you glue firmly (You can also sew parts of it instead of sewing the whole thing)
Simple Method 2 You can draw the pupils, nose, lips, and legs with a fabric pen or a permanent marker if you think stitching them is too hard and don't want to do it

12 There's no rule that says you have to put felt appliqués on fabric Try some variations:
It would be cute to glue felt appliqués on a paper box
It would also be nice to put a color paper appliqué on your notebook

13 You can make appliqués with pictures and words that aren't in this book
Bad handwriting will still come out well.
"White Rabbit" しろうさ
You can make your own appliqué patterns by tracing your favorite pictures onto paper
You can also make appliqué patterns by writing words and outlining them You can even appliqué your name

14 You can turn appliqués into mascots if you stack two, sew them together, and stuff cotton inside If you add a string, it can be a key ring
I can be a mascot.
Cotton
Sew a string to the top part of the back
I can also be a key ring.
Back Front

15 It seems easy. Yes, it's easy.
And also fun! Yes, it's a lot of fun.
Give making appliqués a shot!

73

Fun Appliqué Materials

 Chalk pencils

 Scissors

 **Glue**

Embroidery needle
Used to FN Stitch and S-Stitch pupils, noses, and such

Sewing needle
Used to overlock stitch

Felt
Respective colors

Embroidery thread
Respective colors

Fun Appliqué Patterns

Jumping Rabbit is done

It'll look cute to have a line of them jumping around

Pupil: FN Stitch, turning 3 turns
Red thread, 6 strands

Body, 1 piece
White

Wings, 2 pieces
Red

Beak, 1 piece
Yellow

Body, 1 piece
Red

Face, 1 piece
Red

The angle of my wings makes it seem like I'm flying.

Pupil: FN Stitch, turning 3 times
Black thread, 6 strands

Flying Red Bird is done

Resting Red Bird is done

Tail, 1 piece
Red

Face, 1 piece
Red

Body, 1 piece
Red

Beak, 1 piece
Yellow

It looks nice if you make my back seem slightly rounded.

Pupil: FN Stitch, turning 3 times
Black thread, 6 strands

Foot: S-Stitch
Red thread, 6 strands

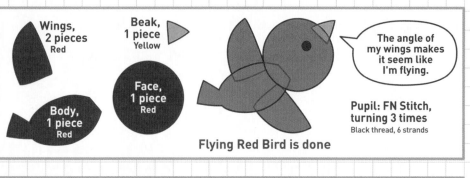

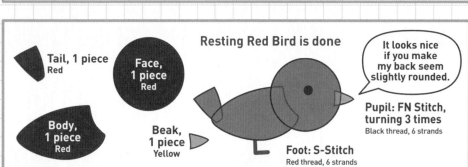

Face, 1 piece
Green

Legs, 4 pieces
Green

Body, 1 piece
Green

Tail, 1 piece
Green

Pupils: FN Stitch, turning once
Black thread, 6 strands

Shell design: S-Stitch
Black thread, 6 strands

Turtle is done

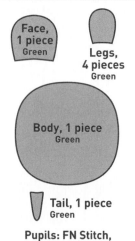

Fun Appliqué Patterns

Face, 1 piece
White

Ears, 2 pieces
White

I want clothes in lots of different colors.

Arms, 2 pieces
White

Clothes, 1 piece
Pink

Legs, 2 pieces
White

Pupils: FN Stitch, turning 3 times
Brown thread, 6 strands

Nose: FN Stitch, turning once
Brown thread, 6 strands

Mouth: S-Stitch
Brown thread, 6 strands

White Rabbit is done

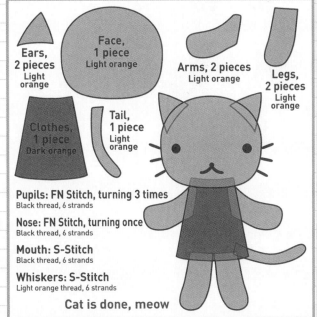

Ears, 2 pieces
Light orange

Face, 1 piece
Light orange

Arms, 2 pieces
Light orange

Legs, 2 pieces
Light orange

Clothes, 1 piece
Dark orange

Tail, 1 piece
Light orange

Pupils: FN Stitch, turning 3 times
Black thread, 6 strands

Nose: FN Stitch, turning once
Black thread, 6 strands

Mouth: S-Stitch
Black thread, 6 strands

Whiskers: S-Stitch
Light orange thread, 6 strands

Cat is done, meow

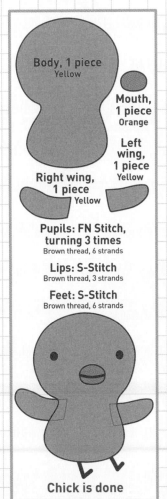

Body, 1 piece
Yellow

Mouth, 1 piece
Orange

Left wing, 1 piece
Yellow

Right wing, 1 piece
Yellow

Pupils: FN Stitch, turning 3 times
Brown thread, 6 strands

Lips: S-Stitch
Brown thread, 3 strands

Feet: S-Stitch
Brown thread, 6 strands

Chick is done

Bobbed hair, 1 piece
Brown

Hair, parted on the side, 1 piece
Brown

You can make a variety of hats and hairstyles with felt and embroidery thread!

Face, 1 piece
Flesh-colored

Hat, 1 piece
In a color of your choice

Clothes, 1 piece
In a color of your choice

Make a boy that looks just like you.

Make a girl that looks just like you.

Pupils: FN Stitch, turning 3 times
Brown thread, 6 strands

Mouth: S-Stitch
Brown thread, 6 strands

Arms, legs: S-Stitch
Thread in same color as clothes, 6 strands

Hair: S-Stitch
Brown thread, 6 strands

Boy and Girl are done

Make an appliqué of any animal that you want.
Make it any size that you want. Use any color felt that you want.
Appliqué on whatever you want, as much as you want.

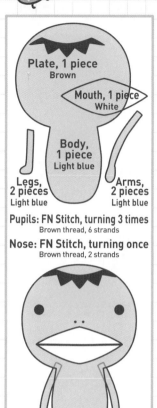

Plate, 1 piece
Brown

Mouth, 1 piece
White

Body, 1 piece
Light blue

Legs, 2 pieces
Light blue

Arms, 2 pieces
Light blue

Pupils: FN Stitch, turning 3 times
Brown thread, 6 strands

Nose: FN Stitch, turning once
Brown thread, 2 strands

Lips: S-Stitch
Light-blue thread, 2 strands

Sprite is done

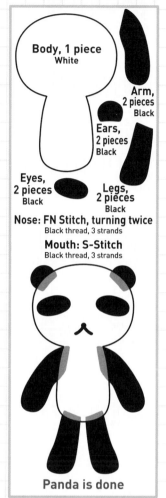

Body, 1 piece
White

Arm, 2 pieces
Black

Ears, 2 pieces
Black

Eyes, 2 pieces
Black

Legs, 2 pieces
Black

Nose: FN Stitch, turning twice
Black thread, 3 strands

Mouth: S-Stitch
Black thread, 3 strands

Panda is done

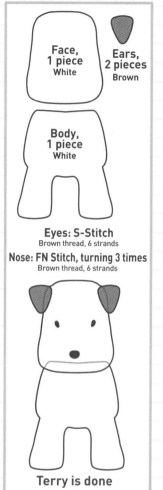

Face, 1 piece
White

Ears, 2 pieces
Brown

Body, 1 piece
White

Eyes: S-Stitch
Brown thread, 6 strands

Nose: FN Stitch, turning 3 times
Brown thread, 6 strands

Terry is done

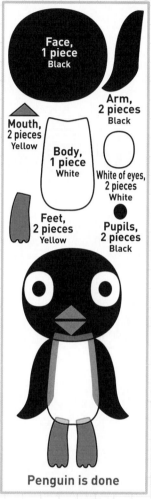

Face, 1 piece
Black

Arm, 2 pieces
Black

Mouth, 2 pieces
Yellow

Body, 1 piece
White

White of eyes, 2 pieces
White

Feet, 2 pieces
Yellow

Pupils, 2 pieces
Black

Penguin is done

Face, 1 piece
Black

Right white of eyes
1 piece
White

Left white of eyes
1 piece
White

Mouth, 1 piece
White

Clothes, 1 piece
Red

Pupils: FN Stitch, turning twice
Black thread, 6 strands

Arms, legs: S-Stitch
Black thread, 6 strands

Bad Guy is done

Ears, 2 pieces
Brown

White of eyes, 2 pieces
White

Muzzle, 1 piece
White

Face, 1 piece
Brown

Arms, 2 pieces
Brown

Legs, 2 pieces
Brown

Clothes, 1 piece
Light blue

Pupils: FN Stitch, turning 3 times
Black thread, 6 strands

Nose: FN Stitch, turning once
Black thread, 6 strands

Mouth: S-Stitch
Black thread, 6 strands

Bear is done

Fun Appliqué Patterns

Face, 1 piece Light green

White of eyes, 2 pieces White

Clothes, 1 piece Dark green

Pupils: FN Stitch, turning 3 times Black thread, 6 strands

Mouth, arms, legs: S-Stitch Light-green thread, 6 strands

Frog is done

Ears, 2 pieces Yellow

Face, 1 piece Yellow

Body, 1 piece Yellow

Tail, 1 piece Yellow

Eyes, nose: FN Stitch, turning twice Black thread, 6 strands

Fox is done

Ears, 2 pieces Flesh-colored

Face, 1 piece Flesh-colored

Nose, 1 piece Flesh-colored

Body, 1 piece Flesh-colored

Legs, 2 pieces Flesh-colored

Arms, 2 pieces Flesh-colored

Eyes: FN Stitch, turning 3 times Brown thread, 6 strands

Nostrils: FN Stitch, turning once Brown thread, 3 strands

Pig is done

Body, 1 piece Brown

Tail, 1 piece Brown

Arm, 1 piece Brown

Face, 1 piece Flesh-colored

Eyes: FN Stitch, turning twice Brown thread, 6 strands

Nose and mouth: S-Stitch Brown thread, 3 strands

Munky is done

You can make a chain of Munkys if you connect their paws and tails (and he's not a "Monkey," okay?)

Let's chain!

Eyes: FN Stitch, turning twice Brown thread, 6 strands

Nose: FN Stitch, turning once Brown thread, 6 strands

Mouth: S-Stitch Brown thread, 6 strands

Pupils: FN Stitch, turning three times Brown thread, 6 strands

Face, 1 piece Flesh-colored

Face, 1 piece Black

Arms, 2 pieces Flesh-colored

Legs, 2 pieces Flesh-colored

White of eyes, 2 pieces White

Arms, 2 pieces Black

Legs, 2 pieces Black

Body, 1 piece White

Horns, 2 pieces White
Cut a notch with scissors along the dotted line

White Sheep and Black Sheep are done

Fun Appliqué Patterns

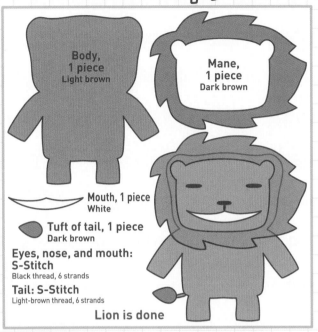

Body, 1 piece
Light brown

Mane, 1 piece
Dark brown

Mouth, 1 piece
White

Tuft of tail, 1 piece
Dark brown

Eyes, nose, and mouth: S-Stitch
Black thread, 6 strands

Tail: S-Stitch
Light-brown thread, 6 strands

Lion is done

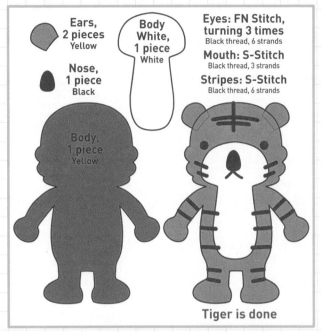

Ears, 2 pieces
Yellow

Nose, 1 piece
Black

Body White, 1 piece
White

Body, 1 piece
Yellow

Eyes: FN Stitch, turning 3 times
Black thread, 6 strands

Mouth: S-Stitch
Black thread, 3 strands

Stripes: S-Stitch
Black thread, 6 strands

Tiger is done

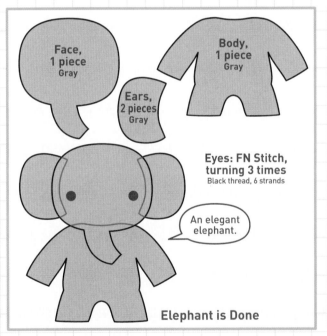

Face, 1 piece
Gray

Body, 1 piece
Gray

Ears, 2 pieces
Gray

Eyes: FN Stitch, turning 3 times
Black thread, 6 strands

An elegant elephant.

Elephant is Done

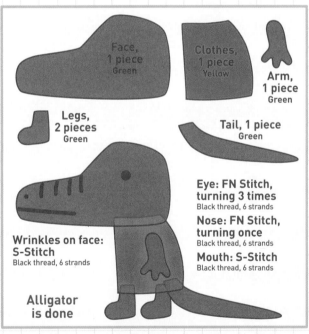

Face, 1 piece
Green

Clothes, 1 piece
Yellow

Arm, 1 piece
Green

Legs, 2 pieces
Green

Tail, 1 piece
Green

Eye: FN Stitch, turning 3 times
Black thread, 6 strands

Nose: FN Stitch, turning once
Black thread, 6 strands

Mouth: S-Stitch
Black thread, 6 strands

Wrinkles on face: S-Stitch
Black thread, 6 strands

Alligator is done

Mouth: S-Stitch
Black thread, 6 strands

Eyes: FN Stitch, turning once
Black thread, 2 strands

S-Stitch
Brown thread, 6 strands

You can connect as many cars as you want!

Additional cars, as many as you like
In a color of your choice

Leading car, 1 piece
In a color of your choice

Pupils: FN Stitch, turning 3 times
Black thread, 6 strands

Wheels
Brown

Windows, as many as required
White

White of eye, 1 piece
White

Train is done

ARANZI ARONZO

Aranzi Aronzo is a company that
"makes what it feels like the way it feels like and then sells the stuff."
Established in 1991 in Osaka. Kinuyo Saito and Yoko Yomura team.
Other than original miscellany, Aranzi Aronzo also makes picture books and exhibits.
Other books include *Cute Dolls, Fun Dolls, The Cute Book, The Bad Book,* and *Aranzi Machine Gun vols. 1-3.*

http://www.aranziaronzo.com
http://www.vertical-inc.com/aranzi_aronzo

Translation — Rui Munakata

Copyright © 2008 by Aranzi Aronzo

All rights reserved.

Published by Vertical, Inc., New York.

Originally published in Japanese as *Kawaii Mochimono*
by Bunka Shuppankyoku, Tokyo, 2005.

ISBN 978-1-934287-09-5

Manufactured in Singapore

First American Edition

Vertical, Inc.
www.vertical-inc.com